YOU CAN TEACH YOURSELF®

MANDOLIN by EAR

By Jack Hatfield

CD Contents

Visit us on the Web at http://www.melbay.com — E-mail us at email@melbay.com

HOW TO READ TABLATURE

Tablature is a way of writing music for stringed instruments that shows you what notes to play graphically instead of by musical notation. Here is how it works:

A staff of mandolin tablature has four lines. Each line represents one of the strings. The first (top) line represents the first (bottom, or E) string. The second (from the top) line represents the second (from the bottom, or A) string, and so on. Remember, the first line represents the *bottom* string, not the *top* string.

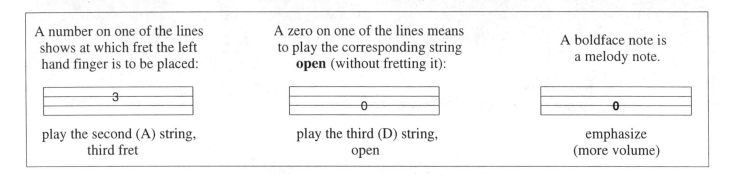

A number on one of the lines shows at which fret the left hand finger is to be placed:	A zero on one of the lines means to play the corresponding string **open** (without fretting it):	A boldface note is a melody note.
play the second (A) string, third fret	play the third (D) string, open	emphasize (more volume)

Timing (note duration) is shown by stems, beams, and flags. If a note stands alone and has a vertical stem, it is a *quarter note*. It lasts <u>one</u> beat. A note whose stem is connected to another note or notes by a bold horizontal beam is an *eighth note*. It lasts <u>one half</u> of a beat. A lone eighth note will have a flag on its stem. All beats are equidistant in time. Therefore, a quarter note lasts exactly twice as long as an eighth note. A dot after a note adds half again value to it *e.g.* - a dotted quarter note lasts <u>one and a half</u> beats. When a note is to last longer than one beat, a *tie* will be used to join two or more notes. Add the total number of beats tied and play as one note. Often notes held longer than one beat are played on the mandolin as a *tremolo*. To perform a tremolo, "fan" the pick rapidly across the string to produce the effect of a sustained note. A tremolo will be shown as a horizontal hash mark on the note stem.

A one-beat silence is a *quarter rest*. It will be shown by a "squiggle" mark. A two-beat silence is a *half rest*. It will be shown by a bold hyphen attached to the third line.

To make it easier to count time and keep your place, the music will be divided into equal segments called *measures* or *bars*. A vertical *bar line* separates the bars (the pickup notes at the beginning of the song will usually be a partial measure). A vertical double line, one regular and one bold, marks the end of the song.

Chord symbols will be in bold caps above the tablature. *Hammer-ons, pull-offs,* and *slides* will be shown as two notes with a bold dash between them and a "h", "p", or "s" underneath. *Melody notes* will be in bold type - they are to be emphasized.

A sample section of tablature appears below with features labeled.

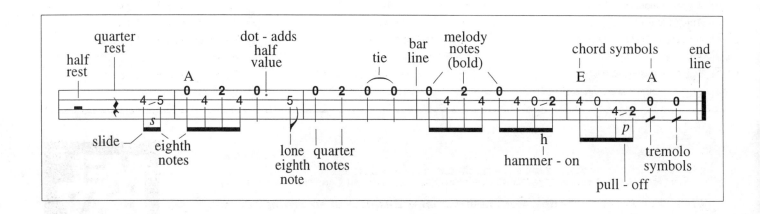

Introduction

Learning to play a musical instrument is one of the most rewarding and satisfying experiences a music lover can have. As any endeavor that is worthwhile, though, it requires a lot of dedication and hard work.

It is very difficult to learn to play a musical instrument without the aid of a teacher or an instruction manual. There are many fine instruction manuals that are designed to make the learning process as efficient as possible via the printed page. Most teachers use these instruction manuals or write their own arrangements for students. Some students prefer to learn with the aid of self-instruction manuals or self-instructing video courses. These video instruction courses usually include tablature books to clarify and inform when a video tape player is not handy. Again, much of the information is conveyed via the printed page.

Though musical notation and tablature are incredibly important tools, they have their pitfalls. Often the student gets so comfortable with the routine of learning from the printed page that he never makes a conscious effort to develop his listening skills. All he can do is play by rote. In other words, the songs are played from memory exactly the same way each time, with no variation or improvisation.

Many musicians, even some that are technically advanced, never break away from the printed music and start teaching themselves to play by simply listening and re-creating. The common name for this process is "playing by ear". To those who have never tried, playing by ear seems like a vast and mysterious no-man's land. Many musicians either lack the necessary confidence or do not believe they are ready to learn by ear. The truth is that any musician with rudimentary skills can teach himself to play by ear if he is aware of some basic guidelines. That is what this book is all about.

It may seem contradictory that a book could teach you to play by ear. The fact is, the tools you need are largely conceptual. There are certain rules and probabilities that govern musical composition. There are also some basic building blocks that songs are composed of. If you are aware of these concepts and conventions, you will become incredibly more adept at playing by ear.

Along with the information, you need two other things: desire and experience. You undoubtedly have the desire or you would not have spent your hard-earned money on this book. You now have access to the information, so grab your mandolin and let's get some experience.

TABLE OF CONTENTS

Chapter 1

LEARNING CHORD PROGRESSIONS BY EAR

In order to learn a song by ear, it is best to begin by learning the chord progression. This will not only help you to figure out the melody later, but will also equip you to play rhythm accompaniment. First, however, let's get a brief overview so you will understand the role played by chords in a musical composition.

Elements of Music

The most basic element of music is the *note*. A note is a specific frequency of sound waves which is experienced by the human ear as a musical pitch. There are twelve notes in our system of music, each separated by an interval of a *half-step* (a one fret interval) or a *whole-step* (a two-fret interval). Using various arrangements of half-step and whole-step intervals, different *scales* can be constructed. The most commonly used scales are the *major scale* and the (melodic) *minor scale*. The *melody* is an interesting arrangement of notes, generally selected from the scale, and played in sequence. *Chords* are formed by selecting three or more notes which have a pleasing harmony and playing these notes simultaneously. Chords not only provide harmony for the melody line, but also create a venue for the rhythm instruments. The scale, its inherent chords, and the relationships therein all go together to define the *key*. Add to these components the organizing aspect of *rhythm*, and you have **music**.

Determining Meter and Counting Time

The most basic element of rhythm is the *beat*. A beat is a steady pulse - like a heartbeat or the ticking of a clock. Unless otherwise indicated by the composer, all beats within a musical composition are equidistant in time. Individual beats are grouped into larger units of equal length. Each one of these units is called a *measure* or *bar*.

The number of beats assigned to each measure is one of the factors that determines the *meter* of a composition. Most music styles that include the mandolin use one of only four meters: 2/4 time, ("march time") 4/4 time ("Common time") 3/4 time ("waltz time") and 6/8 time ("jig time"). For our purposes, any of these meters can be interpreted in 4/4 time or 3/4 time. All tablature examples in this book will be in one of these two meters.

To count 4/4 time, start precisely when the rhythm instruments do and count "One, two, three, four; One, two, three, four . . . "etc. Listen to the words and music for an emphasis or "swell" which marks the first beat of each measure. Listen also for the chord changes - most of them occur on the first beat of a measure. Sing the words to the first line of the sample song *Worried Man Blues* which is shown on the following page. Notice how you automatically emphasize the words "takes", "man", "sing", and "song". These words all coincide with the first beat of a measure.

You should emphasize the first beat when counting time also; "**One,** two, three, four; **One,** two, three, four . . . " etc. This helps create a "marker point", making it easier to keep your place. Continue counting each measure as such, making sure that the musical and/or vocal phrases are synchronized with your counting. If not, you either selected the wrong meter or you did not start counting precisely on the first beat of the first complete measure. Remember, start counting when the **rhythm instruments** start, not when the lead instrument starts. The lead instrument usually starts **before** the first beat of the first full measure.

Counting Pickup Notes

Note that the first word of the lyrics and/or the first note played by an instrumentalist does not always occur on the first beat of a measure. Most songs have *pickup notes* that lead into the first beat and provide a musical signal so the rhythm players can start together. Pickup notes are normally less than a full measure in length - in 4/4 time, they can total one to three beats. In 3/4 time they can total one or two beats. Usually these pickup notes are played or sung by a soloist, and the full band starts playing on the first beat of the first *complete* measure. That is where the chord progression actually starts.

In the first line of the sample song *Worried Man Blues* below, the note that is sung on the word "It" is a pickup note. It occurs on the count of "four", since it is immediately before the "**One**" of the first full measure. The chord progression actually starts on the word "takes" - the first beat of the first complete measure.

Worried Man Blues

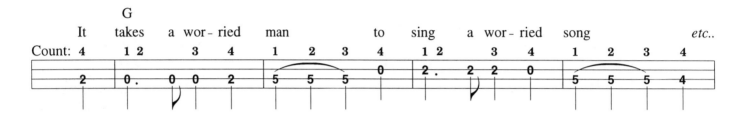

To count in 3/4 time, simply count "**One**, two, three; **One** two, three . . .etc.", again starting with the rhythm instruments and emphasizing "**One**". The first line of *Amazing Grace* is shown below to demonstrate counting in 3/4 time. Listen to the demonstration recording to hear these examples counted.

Amazing Grace

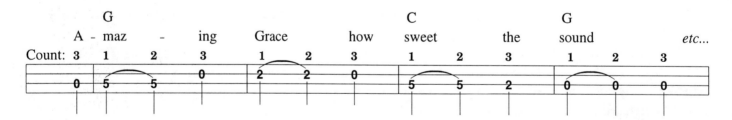

8

Exercise 1

DETERMINING METER

On the demonstration recording that accompanies this book, the melody is on the left channel and the rhythm instruments are on the right. Turn the balance control of your stereo to the middle position so you can get clues from the phrasing of the melody *and* from the changing of the chords. Listen to Progressions # 1 - # 12 near the beginning of the recording. Each example will be played in either 3/4 time or in 4/4 time. Determine the meter and circle the correct answer below. *Answers on page 83.*

1	3/4	4/4	4	3/4	4/4	7	3/4	4/4	10	3/4	4/4
2	3/4	4/4	5	3/4	4/4	8	3/4	4/4	11	3/4	4/4
3	3/4	4/4	6	3/4	4/4	9	3/4	4/4	12	3/4	4/4

Song Parts and Song Form

You learned earlier that beats are grouped into larger units called *measures*. Measures are grouped into still larger units called *song parts*. In an instrumental tune, these are often referred to as the *A part, B part, C part,* etc. In a vocal number, there are typically two song parts: A song part that appears two or more times with the same melody line and chord progression, but non-repeating lyrics, is a *verse*. A song part that appears two or more times with a repeating melody line, chord progression, and lyrics is a *chorus*. The verse and chorus can have the same melody and chord structure, but the repetition or non-repetition of the lyrics can define them as different song parts. The verse is usually sung by a solo vocalist. The chorus often employs vocal harmony. Some songs, particularly ballads, are composed entirely of verses. Vocal harmony is sometimes used on these songs. Some country, swing, jazz, and popular songs contain a third part which only appears once and has melody, lyrics, and chord progression that are unlike the verse or chorus. This song part is called a *bridge*. The bridge usually appears just before the last chorus.

The most common format is a verse and a chorus of eight bars each. A sixteen-bar verse and chorus is also popular. The twelve-bar progression is also common, the twelve-bar blues being a very good example. Usually the twelve-bar progression is either the lone song part or the melody and chord progression of the verse and chorus is identical, with only the lyrics changing.

Most vocal songs also contain *solos*, or *breaks*, consisting of a lone musician playing a song part instrumentally. Sometimes there is a very short solo that has a special function in the song. This mini-solo can come in the form of an *introduction (intro), turnaround,* or *ending*. Intros and turnarounds are usually four measures long, and often identical or very similar to the last four bars of a verse or chorus. Another very common intro for a twelve-bar or sixteen-bar song consists of the first four bars and the last four bars of a verse or chorus combined to form an eight bar intro. In bluegrass, the intro is often a complete verse or chorus. Turnarounds appear at the end of song parts - they "turn you around" to the beginning of the next song part. Turnarounds are very popular in gospel music. Endings can consist of a single strum on the key chord, a two-bar "shave and a haircut", or any number of unique forms. The double "shave and a haircut" is a very common ending for bluegrass instrumentals. Endings are used in practically all forms of music. In gospel and modern country music, the intro, turnaround, and ending are often an identical four-bar phrase.

Locating Chord Changes

We will now try to determine where the chord changes occur in a song. *Most chord changes take place on the first beat of a measure.* Listen to the sample song *Worried Man Blues* on the demonstration recording. Concentrate only on the rhythm instruments. The various instruments combine to form a matrix of sound with a basic tone that can be identified as the *root note* of the chord. The bass is particularly responsible for playing the root note on the first beat of each measure. Listen to the overall sound, but especially listen to the bass on the first beat of each measure to see if the note played is different from the note played on the first beat of the preceding measure. If there is no bass, listen for the bass note of the guitar (or the piano in gospel or country music) on the first beat of the measure. Do not be concerned with naming the chord at this point - we are only trying to determine *where* in the progression the chords change.

Exercise 2

LOCATING SIMPLE CHORD CHANGES

With the balance control of your stereo turned fully to the right, listen again to Progressions #1 - #3 near the beginning of the demonstration recording. In the blank chord charts that follow, each box represents one measure. Note the meter (3/4 time or 4/4 time) in the space provided. Above the diagram, mark a small "x" after the measure line where each chord change occurs. Do not be concerned with the name of the chord now, merely at what point it changes. The sample progression *Worried Man Blues* is worked for you to demonstrate the procedure. *The answers can be found on page 83.*

Verse/Chorus:

Sample Progression
Meter:_____4/4_____

				X		X

			X		X	

Verse/Chorus:

Progression #1:
Meter:_____

Progression #2:
Meter:_____

Verse:

Chorus:

Verse/Chorus:

Progression #3:
Meter:_____

Split-Bar Chord Changes

Sometimes there is more than one chord within a measure. When a measure contains more than one chord it is called a *split bar*. Although listening to the bass is still very important, this alone will not alert you to chord changes with absolute certainty in a split bar situation. This is because (in 4/4 time) the bass usually plays an alternate bass note on the third beat of the measure, or may be playing a "passing tone" that leads to the next chord root. It will often be impossible to distinguish either of these from an actual chord change by listening only to the bass. You must also listen to the other rhythm instruments. *Caution* - Just because there is a lead-in does not necessarily mean that the chord changes on the first beat of the next measure - the bass player can lead to the same chord root as in the preceding measure simply for interest.

In 3/4 time, the bass rarely alternates notes within the measure, so if you hear a different bass note on the third beat, it probably means that a chord change has occurred. However, the bass may alternate notes on the first beat of consecutive measures if there are several measures of the same chord. To be certain whether a chord change has taken place on the first beat of a measure, it will again be necessary to listen to the other rhythm instruments.

Exercise 3

LOCATING SPLIT-BAR CHORD CHANGES

With the balance control of your stereo turned fully to the right, listen again to Progressions #4 - #6 near the beginning of the demonstration recording. In these examples, the chords may change not only on the first beat of the measure, but also within the measure. Each box is already subdivided into the proper number of segments - three segments for 3/4 time and four segments for 4/4 time. Mark a small "x" above the part of the box that corresponds with the location of each chord change. For example, if a chord change occurs on the third beat of a measure, place an "x" above the measure box in the third segment. *The answers appear on page 84.*

Progression #4:
Meter:_____4/4_____

Verse:

Chorus:

Progression #5:
Meter:_____4/4_____

Verse:

Chorus:

Progression #6:
Meter:_____3/4_____

Verse/Chorus:

The Number System

One problem in learning chord progressions using the traditional letter system of naming chords is that most individuals can only play a song in the key they learned it in - they cannot instantly transpose it into other keys. Although a person may know a song well in the learned key, he is lost if he encounters someone who wants to sing or play it in a different key. A musician should be able to think in a format that will allow him to play a song in any key at will.

The letter system can also be a hindrance when a fretted instrument player who is not using a capo is trying to communicate a chord progression to another player who is, or when both are using capos, but at different positions. Though the notes produced are in the same key, the musicians are *thinking* in different keys. For example, a mandolinist may wish to play in the key of E without a capo. The banjoist may choose to play along by capoing at the fourth fret and "thinking" in the key of C, which is a much more familiar position than playing in the key of E while in uncapoed G tuning. The guitarist may choose to capo at the second fret and think in the key of D. When calling out or writing the chords, which key do you use? No matter which of the three keys is chosen, two of the musicians must transpose to the key they are thinking in before they can play the proper chords. Though mandolin players seldom use capos, they often play with banjo, guitar, and dobro players who do. They must be able to communicate with these players in a language that does not require on-the-spot transposing.

Still another limitation of the letter system, the most important for this discussion, is that thinking in a multi-key format makes it harder to understand the fundamental structures and tendencies of musical composition. It is this knowledge of basic musical rules and probabilities that provides clues to the musician who is learning a song by ear. The rules and tendencies of chord progressions are true "across the board" for *all* keys. If you understand a concept in one key, you should understand it in any other key. If you learn a song in one key, you should be able to play it in other keys without having to learn it "from scratch" all over again.

A simpler, more all-encompassing way to communicate information about chords and progressions is to give the notes and chords number names instead of letter names. This system is thousands of years old - it was used in ancient Egypt. It has survived the popularity of the letter system of musical notation and is now being brought back into use by studio and performing musicians. They favor the number system when communicating information about chord progressions because of its usefulness and simplicity.

This does not mean that the letter system is useless. Relating notes on the musical staff to fingerings on an instrument is a very efficient method of showing how to play a melody. The tablature system is also very effective for communicating a melody line. But the letter system and tablature are awkward when it comes to communicating fundamentals of musical composition, especially information about chords and chord progressions. Since that is the goal of this chapter, we will use the number system extensively. However, in giving actual musical examples that you may want to play on your instrument, the letter system will also be used. Hopefully by the time you have worked through this book, thinking in terms of the number system will be second nature to you.

How the Number System Works

Each major key is based on a major scale which has seven degrees or *notes*. Think of *do, re, mi, fa, so, la* and *ti*. Instead of assigning these notes letter names, we will assign them the number names 1 through 7. *Note* - In the text of this book, individual note names and key names will be in plain type (A, E, 2, 6) and chord names will be in boldface type (**A, E^7 2, 6m**) for clarity.

We will use the key of G major to demonstrate, because it is one of the most popular keys in music styles that include the mandolin. Since the G note is the first degree of the G major scale, we will assign it the number 1. The A note is the second degree of the G major scale, so it becomes the number 2. The B note, being the third note of the scale, becomes the number 3, and so on until all seven tones of the scale are assigned a number name:

THE G MAJOR SCALE

Letter name:	G	A	B	C	D	E	F♯
Number name:	1	2	3	4	5	6	7

It is a simple matter to extend the number naming system to chords. Each of the scale tones above can be the root of several different chords. Any G-rooted chord in the key of G major would be referred to as a **1** chord: the **G** chord would be called the **1** chord; the **Gm** chord would be called the **1m** chord; the **G^7** chord would be called the **1^7** chord. The **A, Am,** or **A^7** chord would be called the **2, 2m,** or **2^7** chord. The **B, Bm,** or **B^7** chord would be called the **3, 3m,** or **3^7** chord, and so on.

Now let us expand our use of the number system to other keys. The transposition chart on the following page shows the chords for the seven "natural" keys and their corresponding number names. To transpose a given chord progression from the letter system to the number system, locate the key in the first vertical column. The basic chords that are in that key will extend in a row to the right of the key name. Locate the letter name of each chord in the song and look vertically up the column. The number name for that chord will appear at the top of the column.

The transposition chart can also be used to transpose songs from the number system into the letter system. Simply reverse the process: Find the number of the chord in the first line of the chart, and trace it vertically down the column to the row of the desired key to find its letter name in that key.

Remember that the ultimate goal is to reach the point that you can transpose from letters to numbers and vice versa instantly without using the chart. This will eliminate delays, mistakes, and panic when communicating chord progressions in a jam session or band practice. Devote some personal practice time to transposing between numbers and letters, becoming so fluent that on-the-spot transposing in real playing situations becomes instantaneous. After a few attempts using the chart, practice transposing without it, using it only to check your work. You can refer to your repertoire or to songbooks for sample progressions to help you practice transposing from the letter system to the number system and vice versa.

LETTER SYSTEM/NUMBER SYSTEM TRANSPOSITION CHART

NUMBER NAME →	1	2 m or 7	3 m or 7	4	5 or 57	6 m or 7	7°
KEY ↓			LETTER NAME				
C	C	Dm or 7	Em or 7	F	G or G7	Am or 7	B°
D	D	Em or 7	F♯m or 7	G	A or A7	Bm or 7	C♯°
E	E	F♯m or 7	G♯m or 7	A	B or B7	C♯m or 7	D♯°
F	F	Gm or 7	Am or 7	B♭	C or C7	Dm or 7	E°
G	G	Am or 7	Bm or 7	C	D or D7	Em or 7	F♯°
A	A	Bm or 7	C♯m or 7	D	E or E7	F♯m or 7	G♯°
B	B	C♯m or 7	D♯m or 7	E	F♯ or F♯7	G♯m or 7	A♯°

Identifying the Key

The first step in actually figuring out the chords to a song is identifying the key. It is a good idea to first listen through the entire song with your instrument in hand. Song parts almost always end with the key chord. Focus on the last melody note and the bass note of the last chord in the verses and choruses, especially the last chord of the song. The process of guessing the key is basically one of trial-and-error. You must play the various notes in the musical alphabet on your instrument one at a time until you find the one that matches the last melody note and bass note of the song parts. This is the key note of the song.

Including the sharps and flats, there is a total of twelve notes in our musical alphabet. However, if you play bluegrass, folk, country, gospel, or old-time music, the most common keys that you will play in are G, A, C, D, E, and F, roughly in that order of popularity. Guess these notes in the prescribed order, and you will usually identify the key in no more than three or four tries. If you play bluegrass music, especially if the lead singer has a high-pitched voice, you may also play in the keys of B and B♭. The other "sharp keys" and "flat keys" are seldom used in string band music. Many female singers favor keys from B♭ to D, and will occasionally require you to play in sharp or flat keys within this range.

The Diatonic Triads

A three-note stack of major third or minor third intervals can be constructed using each of the seven major scale tones as a root note. (The *root note* is the note that names the chord. For example, the root of a **Gm** chord is the G note. The root of a **D⁷** chord is the D note.) These chords are called the *diatonic triads*. They are by far the most likely chords that will be used in a given key. In learning chord progressions by ear, you can think of the diatonic triads as a palette to draw from when guessing unknown chords.

The Diatonic Triads

	1	2m	3m	4	5	6m	7°
Number System:	1	2m	3m	4	5	6m	7°
Letter System, Key of G:	G	Am	Bm	C	D	Em	F#°

The Three Basic Chords

Some of the diatonic triads are used more frequently than others. The chords that are built on the **1, 4** and **5** degrees of the major scale are by far the most popular. Over seventy-five percent of all bluegrass, folk, gospel, old-time and traditional country songs are composed of only these three chords. The letter names of the three basic chords depend on the key that is being used. In the key of G, they are the **G, C** and **D (or D⁷)** chords. The transposition chart on page 15 can be used to identify the three basic chords in other keys.

Functions of the Three Basic Chords

Once you have determined the key, the next step in learning a song by ear is to identify the three basic chords. We will now examine the function of these chords in order to gain insights that will help us recognize them more easily when we hear them in a song.

The **1** chord functions as the "home base" of the chord progression. The **1** chord is called the *tonic*. In the key of G, the **1** chord is the **G** chord. As you listen to the chords in a song, think of yourself as a traveler on a round trip journey. The **1** chord is usually the starting point and practically always the final destination of a song part or a phrase within the song part. The other chords in the progression can be considered either interesting stops along the way or alternate routes back "home" to the **1** chord which will end the phrase or song part. When you arrive at the **1** chord "destination", it is often like a musical period at the end of a sentence. There is a sense of finality - of an idea having been completed. There is virtually always a pause in the lyrics as a musical phrase or a complete lyrical sentence ends. If you listen to the music and the lyrics with this in mind, you can probably pick out many of the **1** chords in a song. Since the **1** chord has this important function, it is naturally the most frequently occurring chord in most progressions. This is a very important concept to remember - we will be using the laws of probabilities often to reduce the amount of guesswork necessary to identify chords.

The **5** chord is known as the *dominant* chord (The **D** chord in the key of G). It is the next most frequently visited destination of our musical "traveler". Think of the **5** chord as having the strongest attraction, pulling our traveler away from the initial **1** chord. The most basic progression consists of just the **1** chord and the **5** chord. Some well-known examples of **1 - 5** songs are *Oh, My Darling, Clementine,* and *Train '45*. (There *are* one-chord songs, mostly children's songs such as *Three Blind Mice* and *Frere Jaque,* but we will not consider them, since the chords do not change, or "progress".) *Note* - the **5** chord is often voiced as a **5^7** when it occurs just before the final **1** chord in a phrase or song part.

The **4** chord is the next most frequently used chord. It is known as the *subdominant* chord (the **C** chord in the key of G). It appears almost as frequently as the **5** chord, typically in songs that are comprised of three chords or more. It rarely appears as the "other chord" in a two-chord progression. This can be a valuable clue in itself. If you are trying to figure out a song that has three distinct chord sounds in it and you can identify the **1** and **5** chords, it is extremely likely that the other chord is the **4** chord. Another clue - on the occasion that a song part does not start on the **1** chord, it frequently starts on the **4** chord. This is often the case with the second song part in a song. For example, when a song starts with a verse followed by a chorus, the chorus often begins with a **4** chord. When the song starts with a chorus and is followed by a verse, the verse frequently begins with a **4** chord.

Listening For Repetition

Most melody lines and chord progressions involve repetition. If a melody line is repeated, then the chances are extremely good that the accompanying chord progression is also being repeated. Knowing this can save a lot of work. Before beginning to learn a chord progression by ear, listen to the song a few times. Focus on the melody if it is an instrumental tune. Focus on the melody *and* the lyrics if it is a vocal song. Every time you hear a given lyrical phrase, the chords that accompany it may repeat. If the lyrics *and* the accompanying melody line repeat, it is virtually a certainty that the chords repeat also.

Repetition of shorter phrases within the song part is also very common. In 4/4 time, song parts are usually eight measures in length. The component phrases are generally two measures or four measures. Progression # 5 illustrates this. Listen to the recorded example. In the verse there is repetition of a theme every two measures. We will call measures one and two Phrase A. Measures three and four repeat, but not exactly. We will call them Phrase B. Measures five and six are an exact repetition of Phrase A. Measures seven and eight are a new sequence - we will designate them Phrase C.

	Phrase A		Phrase B		Phrase A		Phrase C	
Progression #5 Verse:	G	G C	G	G D	G	G C	G	D G

This eight-measure verse is composed of three two-measure phrases - in recognizing repetition we have eliminated *one fourth* of the work.

Listen to the chorus part of the same progression. It can be broken down into two four-measure phrases, which we will call Phrase D. By recognizing repetition, the work of deducing the chords has been reduced by *half* in the chorus:

	Phrase D				Phrase D			
Progression #5 Chorus:	G			D G	G			D G

17

There are many songs in which the chord progressions of the entire verse and chorus are identical. In other words, the lyrics and presence or absence of vocal harmony is the only difference in the two song parts - the melody and chord progression are the same. In these cases, figuring out the first song part gives you the chords to the entire song. In our ongoing examples, Progression #1, Progression #3, and Progression #6 are examples of this. With the balance control of your stereo adjusted to the middle position, listen to these examples, noting the repetition of melody and chord structure.

We can now devise a step-by-step procedure for learning "basic three" progressions by ear:

LEARNING "BASIC THREE" PROGRESSIONS BY EAR: A STEP-BY-STEP PROCEDURE

1) Determine the key note. Listen to the last melody note and chord root in the song parts. Listen especially to the final melody note and chord root of the song. Use the process of elimination and laws of probability: Guess in the following order: **G, A, C, D, E, F, B.**

2) Determine the 1, 4, and 5 chords of the chosen key. This will be your basic palette from which to choose likely chords. Use the transposition chart on page 15 if necessary.

3) Identify repetition of melody and/or lyrics. If you detect repetition, you may want to mark the repeated phrases on a blank chord chart in advance (Phrase A, Phrase B, etc.).

4) Identify each chord, one by one. Start the recording, stopping it immediately after the first chord. You must learn to focus on the sound of this chord until you can check its identity with your instrument. This will be difficult if the recording is allowed to proceed to the next chord. Guess the identity of the first chord, using the process of elimination and the laws of probability. In other words, guess the **1** chord first. Play the **1** chord on your instrument, listening to see if it matches the sound on the tape, paying special attention to the bass note. If it does not sound like a **1** chord, try the next most likely choice, the **5** chord. If the **1** and **5** chords can be eliminated, the "mystery chord" is almost certainly the **4** chord.

5) Fill in the blank chord chart and proceed to the next chord. Remember, there are only three basic chords. Therefore, once you have identified a chord, you only have two possible choices for the following chord. Remember, also - song parts frequently start on the **1** chord and virtually always end on the **1** chord. If the song part does not start on the **1** chord, the **4** chord is the next most probable, followed by the **5** chord. If a chord's identity eludes you, leave that part of the chord chart blank and go on. You may identify chord sequences later in the song that are the same or similar, giving you clues as to the problem chord.

6) Listen again for repetition. After identifying the first few changes, listen again to the lyrics and melody line to see if earlier phrases reappear. Note any repetition on the chart.

7) Check your work. When you are finished, listen again to the entire song, playing along on your instrument. If you hear mistakes, rework the problem areas.

Exercise 4

LEARNING "BASIC THREE" PROGRESSIONS BY EAR

With the balance control of your stereo adjusted to the middle position, listen again to the melody and chord progressions of Progressions #1 - #6 (program numbers 4 - 9 on the recording), for which you have already determined the meter and location of the chord changes. Use the step-by-step procedure to identify the chords. Fill in the chord charts on pages 10 - 12. *Answers on pages 84 - 85.*

The Supporting Chords

The chords that appear in the **2, 3,** and **6** positions of the diatonic chord scale can be thought of as the *supporting chords*, much like the supporting actors in a movie. In formal music, these chords are usually voiced as minor or dominant seventh types. However, in mandolin-related styles such as bluegrass, folk, old-time and traditional country music, they are often voiced as major types. If you do hear the minor or seventh quality in a chord, however, there is a strong probability that it is a **2, 3,** or **6** chord.

Note - The **7** chord is used so rarely in music forms that include the mandolin that it can be eliminated from our list of possible chords, making the guesswork easier. It will not be used in any songs or exercises in this book.

Recognizing Chord Types

The next step in learning chord progressions by ear is to learn to identify the type of a given chord. By *type* we mean simply whether a chord is a major, minor, seventh, etc. Each of these chord types has its own unique qualities that can be easily discerned. The various chord types serve only a few basic functions and show up in fairly predictable combinations within a chord progression. By knowing what these functions and combinations are, you can simplify the guesswork immensely when learning a song by ear. You can often deduce a chord's letter name if you can identify its type. For example, if you know a chord is a major type, then it is probably a **1, 4** or **5** chord. If it is a minor type, it is very likely a **2, 3** or **6** chord. By recognizing the type of a chord, you have reduced your palette of possibilities to only three chords, making the guesswork much easier.

There are two primary qualities that chords possess. Being able to identify these qualities will help you determine the chord type. The first quality has to do with what kind of mood or emotion a chord evokes in the listener.

Emotional Characteristics of Chord Types

A major type chord evokes a happy, bright or carefree mood. Play a **G major** chord and listen for the happy, bright quality that it evokes.

A minor type chord evokes a sad, somber or serious mood. Play a **G minor** chord, comparing it to the **G major** chord just played. Can you hear the sad quality of the **Gm**?

A (dominant) seventh type chord evokes a tense or uneasy mood in the listener. Play a **G⁷** chord, noting the feeling of unrest it creates.

These qualities are true for any chord, regardless of its letter name. The emotional characteristics are fairly obvious once you know to listen for them. It is a short leap from being aware of a chord's emotional quality to being able to identify its type.

Consonance and Dissonance

The other quality that can be discerned in a chord is the degree of consonance or dissonance created by the component notes. A *consonant* harmony is a pleasant one. A *dissonant* harmony is an unpleasant or harsh one.

Play a G note and then a B note. Play the two simultaneously. The interval between the two notes is a *major third*, a consonant interval. This is the defining interval of a major triad, in this case a **G major triad.**

MAJOR THIRD INTERVAL (CONSONANT)

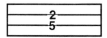

Now play the same G note, followed by a B♭ note. This interval is a *minor third.* It is perceived to be consonant, though perhaps slightly less pleasant than a major third. The minor third is the defining interval of a minor triad, in this case a **G minor triad**.

MINOR THIRD INTERVAL (MILDLY DISSONANT)

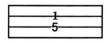

Play a B note, then play an F note. This is a *tritone* interval, which is one of the more unpleasant, or dissonant intervals. This is one of the defining intervals of a seventh chord, in this case, a **G⁷chord.**

TRITONE INTERVAL (VERY DISSONANT)

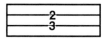

What has just been demonstrated is three varying degrees of consonance (or dissonance). Recognizing this will help you determine whether a chord is of a major, minor or seventh type. Major chords have the most pleasant harmony. Minor chords are slightly less pleasant, but certainly not harsh. Seventh chords have the most unpleasant harmony - one that actually creates uneasiness in the listener.

Of course these are not the only intervals in these chords. There are three notes in the major and minor triad, and four notes in the seventh chord. The distance between any two of these notes is an interval. We have merely focused on the interval that is most responsible for the character of the major, minor and seventh chord types to help you identify them in a song.

If you pay attention to the emotional quality and listen for the amount of consonance or dissonance within a chord, you should be able to determine whether any chord is a major, minor, or seventh type. With just a little practice, even non-musicians can identify major, minor and seventh chords by listening for the emotional aspect alone.

Exercise 5

IDENTIFYING MAJOR, MINOR AND SEVENTH CHORD TYPES

On the demonstration recording that accompanies this book (program number 12 on the recording), listen to the examples for this exercise. A chord will be played on the mandolin. Do not be concerned with the letter name of the chord. Listen for the emotional characteristics and the degree of consonance or dissonance and determine whether the chord is of the A) *major*, B) *minor*, or C) *seventh* type. Circle the correct answer. *The answers can be found on page 86.*

1	A	B	C		21	A	B	C
2	A	B	C		22	A	B	C
3	A	B	C		23	A	B	C
4	A	B	C		24	A	B	C
5	A	B	C		25	A	B	C
6	A	B	C		26	A	B	C
7	A	B	C		27	A	B	C
8	A	B	C		28	A	B	C
9	A	B	C		29	A	B	C
10	A	B	C		30	A	B	C
11	A	B	C		31	A	B	C
12	A	B	C		32	A	B	C
13	A	B	C		33	A	B	C
14	A	B	C		34	A	B	C
15	A	B	C		35	A	B	C
16	A	B	C		36	A	B	C
17	A	B	C		37	A	B	C
18	A	B	C		38	A	B	C
19	A	B	C		39	A	B	C
20	A	B	C		40	A	B	C

The Modal Supporting Chords

The 7♭ **major** chord and the 3♭ **major** chord are the *modal supporting chords*. In the key of G these are the F and the B♭ chords. They are generated not from the key scale, but by a particular *mode* of that scale. A mode can be thought of as an "offshoot" major scale built on each step of the key scale. Modal melody phrases frequently suggest the use of chords other than the diatonic triads and seventh chords. The 7♭ **major** chord and the 3♭ **major** chord lend a bluesy or melancholy feel, making them fairly easy to discern.

Functions of the Supporting Chords

When the supporting chords appear, they can serve one or more of three functions:
a) to *embellish* the chord progression, providing more interest,
b) to act as a *transition* or stepping stone from one chord to another, or
c) as a functional *substitute* for one of the basic three chords.

Embellishment

Supporting chords can be inserted between basic chord changes or in place of basic chords to "spice up" an otherwise simple or predictable progression. The **6m** and the **3m** chords are often used in place of the **1** chord for this purpose. In the key of G, these are the **Em** and the **Bm** chords, respectively. The **G** chord in measure thirteen of *Amazing Grace* below was changed to an **Em** chord to demonstrate. The **Em** chord harmonizes the melody nicely and provides interest to an otherwise predictable progression:

Amazing Grace - Basic Progression

G G C G   G G D D   G G C G   G D G G

Amazing Grace - 6m Chord Functioning as 1 Chord

G G C G   G G D D   G G C G   Em D G G

Seventh chords are sometimes used instead of major chords to lend a bluesy or jazzy atmosphere or to create tension. Contrast the difference in the twelve-bar blues progression using all major chords to the same progression using seventh chords:

Twelve-Bar Blues -All Major Chords

G G G G   C C G G   D D G G

Twelve-Bar Blues - All Seventh Chords

G^7 G^7 G^7 G^7 C^7 C^7 G^7 G^7 D^7 D^7 G^7 G^7

Transitions

Another function of the supporting chords is to act as *transitions* or "stepping stones" between two basic chords. For example, a change from the **1** chord to the **5** chord can be made more interesting and less abrupt if you insert the **2** chord before the **5** chord, as in measure six of *Amazing Grace* below. Listen carefully and you will understand what is meant by the term "transition" - the **A** chord seems to lead the ear from the **G** chord to the **D** chord.

Amazing Grace - 2 Chord Serving as Transition

G G C G   G A D D   G G C G   G D G G

The transitional **2** chord can be voiced as a seventh chord for greater effect. The intervals contained in the dominant seventh chord produce internal dynamics that cause it to "pull" more strongly to the **5** chord.

Amazing Grace - 2^7 Chord Serving as Transition

G G C G   G A^7 D D   G G C G   G D G G

Movement In Fourths and the Dominant Seventh Chord

We are now going to explore the idea of transition further by learning about the dominant seventh chord type and a kind of chord progression logic that is completely different from "basic three" movement. The dominant seventh chord (commonly referred to as simply "seventh" chord) functions primarily as a transition chord. Because of the dissonant intervals in the chord, the listener's mind does not want to remain focused on the it for long. It wants the chords to change or *resolve* to a more pleasant sound.

Play a **D7** chord. Notice the tension. Now play a **G** major chord. *Aah . . . !* In the **G** chord can be felt a release of the tension created by the **D7** chord. This is how seventh chords work to create movement within a chord progression. In a chord change from **D** major to **G** major, more excitement can be generated if you change the last measure or two of the **D** major to a **D7**. Play the following chord progression:

D - D - G - G

Substitute the second measure of the **D** chord with a **D7**, and you will hear the more pronounced sense of movement:

D - D7 - G - G

The seventh chord not only creates movement, it creates *predictable* movement. Because of the internal dynamics of the chord, the dominant seventh chord leads four positions up the musical alphabet. For example, the **D7** chord leads four positions up to a **G** - rooted chord. (**D, E, F, G**). By "**G** - rooted" chord we mean any chord that uses a **G** note as its naming note. It may be a **G** major, a **G** minor, a **G7**, etc. A **G7** chord leads four notes up the musical alphabet to a **C** - rooted chord (**G, A, B, C**), and so on.

The seven-letter musical alphabet is shown below in several octaves to demonstrate its cyclic nature which means chords can move "up a fourth" *ad infinitum.*

A B C D E F G A B C D E F G A B C D E F G A B C D E F G...

This idea is very important when trying to figure out progressions by ear. When your ear tells you that the "mystery chord" is a seventh type, you have a clue as to the probable root of the next chord! Simply count four degrees up the musical alphabet to determine the root name of the next chord. Then identify the type of the mystery chord by listening to the emotional characteristics and degree of consonance or dissonance.

Though the seventh chords appear diatonically as the **2, 3** or **6** chord, any chord can be voiced as a seventh when it is used to signal movement "up a fourth". For example, though the **G** chord is commonly played as a major type in the key of **G** major, it can be voiced as a **G7** when it is followed by a **C** chord. Similarly, the **D** chord can be voiced as **D7** chord when followed by a **G** chord. A **C** chord can be voiced as a **C7** when it precedes an **F** chord.

Substitutions

Note that it is not necessary for all of the "basic three" chords to be present in order for one or more of the supporting chords to be used. A progression can contain only three chords and still include a supporting chord. When this occurs, the supporting chord can usually be viewed as a functional substitute for one of the "basic three" chords.

Often in blues, bluegrass, country, contemporary gospel, and old-time music the **7♭** chord is used as a substitute for a **5** chord. The traditional square dance tune *Old Joe Clark* is an example. In the original old-time version, the verse and chorus were identical, containing only the **1, 4,** and **5** chords. At some point the modal supporting chord **7♭** was inserted to substitute for an **5** chord in the chorus. Both choices harmonize with the melody line, but the use of the **7♭** chord in the chorus adds interest. The use of the **7♭** chord in *Old Joe Clark* became popular and is now considered by most musicians to be the "standard" version. *Note* - We demonstrate in the key of **G** for continuity within this discussion. *Old Joe Clark* is commonly played in the key of **A**.

Old Joe Clark

Verse:		G	G	G	D	G	G	G/D	G
		G	G	G	D	G	G	G/D	G
					*				
Chorus:		G	G	G	F	G	G	G/D	G
					*				
		G	G	G	F	G	G	G/D	G

* chord substitution

The **6m** chord can used as a substitute for the **1** chord or the **4** chord. Since two of its three notes are common to both chords, it harmonizes many of the same melody situations. We demonstrated the use of the **6m** as a substitute for the **1** chord with the song *Amazing Grace* earlier in this chapter. To show how the **6m** can serve as a functional substitute for the **4** chord, consider the progression of *Lonesome Road Blues* below:

Lonesome Road Blues

G	G	G	G	C	C	G	G
C	C	G	G	D	D	G	G

Replace the **4** chords (**C**) with **6m** chords (**Em**), and you have *Foggy Mountain Breakdown*:

Foggy Mountain Breakdown

				*	*		
G	G	G	G	Em	Em	G	G
*	*						
Em	Em	G	G	D	D	G	G

* chord substitution

We can carry this idea a step further by studying the chord progression of *Bluegrass Breakdown*. In this three-part instrumental, the same kind of substitution is employed, using the **7♭** chord (**F**) to function as a **4** chord (**C**) in the first two parts.

Bluegrass Breakdown

A Part:

				*	*		
G	G	G	G	F	F	G	G
*	*						
F	F	G	G	D	D	G	G

B Part:

				*	*		
G	G	G	G	F	F	G	G
*	*						
F	F	G	G	D	D	G	G

C Part:

G	G	G	G	C	C	G	G
C	C	G	G	D	D	G	G

* chord substitution

Functionally, these three chord progressions are all the same. The role of the **4** chord (**C**) is played by the **6m** chord (**Em**) in *Foggy Mountain Breakdown* and by the **7♭** chord (**F**) in the A and B part of *Bluegrass Breakdown*. Both songs are based on the *Lonesome Road Blues* format. If you study your repertoire, you may be surprised to find that there are several recurring formats. Often the chord structure is identical, with no substitutions. For example, *New River Train, Roll in My Sweet Baby's Arms,* and *Mama Don't Allow* have the same progression (and practically the same melody). Recognizing "generic" progressions like these

25

will help you learn new songs by ear. You can even interchange breaks or backup arrangements to play an "unfamiliar" song instantly in a jam session!

The examples on the previous pages show that the only chord that is absolutely essential to the three-chord format is the **1** chord. The **4** and the **5** chords can be replaced with supporting chords. If you realize this, many of the songs that contain supporting chords may make more sense to you. They may be functionally the same as "basic three" songs, but a supporting chord may be doing the work of a "basic three" chord.

Remember, to qualify as a substitute the supporting chord must harmonize well with the melody line. *Caution* - Though experimenting with substitutions is fun and educational, it is not advised that you do so in a jam session or organized group unless the whole group is "in on it". We are studying substitutions merely to help you understand chord functions so it will be easier to identify chords by ear.

Listed below are common supporting chord substitutions for "basic three" chords.

Substitutes for **1** chord: **6m, 3m, 1⁷ when followed by a 4 chord**

Substitutes for **4** chord: **7♭, 2m, 6m**

Substitutes for **5** chord: **2m, 7♭, 3m, 5⁷ when followed by a 1 chord**

Using the Law of Probabilities

Among the chords discussed so far, we have discovered some clear-cut probabilities. If you only hear three chords in a song, they are probably the **1, 4** and **5** chords. It was shown that of these basic three chords, the **1** chord is the most likely to occur. The **5** chord is next most likely, followed by the **4** chord. Knowing these probabilities allows you to eliminate a considerable amount of guesswork when trying to identify an unknown chord. Simply guess the most probable chord first. If that guess is incorrect, guess the next most probable chord, and so on.

If a song part does not start on the **1** chord, it is extremely likely that it starts on the **4** chord. Therefore, if the chord is heard to change at the beginning of a song part (the previous part will virtually always end on the **1** chord), always try the **4** chord as your first guess.

Of the supporting chords, the **2** and **6** chords are most likely to appear, followed by the **7♭** chord. The **3** chord and the **3♭** chord are less likely, but do appear occasionally. Remember, in "theoretically correct" music the **2, 6** and **3** chords are generally played as minor or seventh types, but in traditional music styles, they are often played as major types.

Using the Chord Type as a Clue

The chord function probability chart is reprinted on the following page. If you are having trouble guessing a particular chord by the probability method alone, you can use its *type* as a clue to its *function*, which will help you determine its *name*.

We learned that the basic three chords are most commonly voiced as major types. Therefore, if you determine that a chord is of a major type, it is likely a **1, 4** or **5** chord, in that order of probability. We also learned that the diatonic supporting chords are often minor or seventh types. This means that if you determine that a certain unknown chord is of the minor type, it is likely an **6, 2** or **3** chord, in that order of probability. If the unknown chord is a seventh chord, it can be a **2⁷, 6⁷** or **3⁷** chord, in that order of probability. Remember, a **1, 4** or **5** chord can also be a seventh chord if it is followed by a chord that is a fourth higher - sometimes it is necessary to go one chord further in the progression to find clues that will help you identify a chord. Remember also that seventh chords can be used merely for atmosphere or to set the mood, when a bluesy or jazzy feel is indicated.

As mentioned earlier, in traditional music forms, the supporting chords are often played as major types. Therefore, if an unknown chord is a major type but does not seem to be either a **1, 4,** or **5** chord, guess **2, 6,** or **3** chord, in that order.

Use the chord function probability chart and the chord type probability chart below to help you make more educated guesses when learning a progression by ear.

Note - In order to simplify the difficult study of chord relationships, we have used the one key (the key of G major) for all exercises in the first part of this book. The following charts are presented in the number system so you can use this information in *any* key.

Chord Function Probability Chart

1,   5,   4,   (2, 2m, or 2^7),   (6, 6m, or 6^7), $7\flat$, (3, 3m or 3^7), $3\flat$

Most - used Chords   **Least - used Chords**

Chord Type Probability Chart

If a chord is of the major type, guess the following, in this order of probability:

1	5	4	2	6	$7\flat$	3	$3\flat$

If a chord is of the minor type, guess the following, in this order of probability:

6m	2m	3m	4m	1m	5m

If a chord is of the seventh type, guess the following, in this order of probability:

5^7	2^7	1^7	6^7	4^7	3^7

Note - For a much more detailed study of the concepts presented in this chapter, purchase *How to Play By Ear* by Jack Hatfield. See ad page in the back of this book.

Exercise 6

LEARNING PROGRESSIONS CONTAINING ONE SUPPORTING CHORD

Return to the Sample Progressions (program numbers 14, 15 and 16 on the demonstration recording). Turn the balance control of your stereo to the middle position so you can hear the melody and the chord progression. Progressions #7 - #9 may contain any or all of the "basic three" chords plus one of the supporting chords, the 2 (2m or 2^7), 6 (6m or 6^7), 7♭, 3 (3^7 or 3m), or 3♭. First, determine the location of the chord changes, then use the transposition chart on page 15 to help you determine each chord's letter name. Identify the letter name of each chord, using the probability charts on page 27 as a guide. Remember to listen for emotional characteristics and consonance or dissonance to give you clues about the chord type. Write the chord names in the appropriate boxes below. *The answers can be found on page 86.*

Progression #7:
Meter:_____4/4_____
Key:_____G_____

Verse/Chorus:

Progression #8:
Meter:_____4/4_____
Key: _____G_____

Verse/Chorus:

Progression #9:
Meter:_____4/4_____
Key: _____G_____

Verse:

Chorus:

Exercise 7

LEARNING PROGRESSIONS CONTAINING TWO SUPPORTING CHORDS

Return to the Sample Progressions (program numbers 17, 18 and 19 on the demonstration recording). Turn the balance control of your stereo to the middle position so you can hear the melody and the chord progression. Progressions #10 - #12 may contain any or all of the "basic three" chords plus two supporting chords, the 2 (2m or 27), 6 (6m or 6⁷), 7♭, 3 (3⁷ or 3m), or 3♭. First, determine the location of the chord changes, then use the transposition chart on page 15 to help you determine each chord's letter name. Identify the letter name of each chord, using the probability charts on page 27 as a guide. Write the chord names in the appropriate boxes below. *The answers can be found on page 87.*

Progression #10:
Meter:_____4/4_____
Key:_____G_____

Verse/Chorus:

Progression #11:
Meter:_____4/4_____
Key:_____G_____

Verse/Chorus:

Progression #12:
Meter:_____4/4_____
Key:_____G_____

Verse/Chorus:

Use the blank chord charts below as additional space to work the exercises or to chart other songs of your choice.

Title: _____
Meter: _____
Key: _____

Title: _____
Meter: _____
Key: _____

Title: _____
Meter: _____
Key: _____

Chapter 2

PLAYING THE MELODY BY EAR

Now that you know how to figure out chord progressions, we can proceed to learning melodies by ear. In Chapter 1 you learned to count time and identify the first beat of each measure. The first beat of the measure is important not only because it coincides with most of the chord changes, but also because that is where the most important melody notes occur. If you can duplicate the melody notes that occur on the first beat of each measure, your solo will be recognizable to most listeners. You can then build on this basic arrangement, adding other important melody notes as you become more familiar with the song.

But how do you identify those melody notes? In Chapter 1 we formulated a palette of possible chords that may appear in a given key. It would help to also have a palette of notes to draw from when identifying the melody. For this, we will look to the *scale*.

The Scale

In Chapter 1, you learned about the scale, a group of "legal" notes that can be used to create melodies. Each key has it's associated scale. The naming note (the 1 note) of the scale is the same letter name as the naming note of the key. For example, the G major scale is associated with the key of G major. Two octaves of G major scale notes are shown below, with the 1 notes (G notes) circled. Memorize the location of these notes on your mandolin.

G MAJOR SCALE NOTES IN THE FIRST POSITION

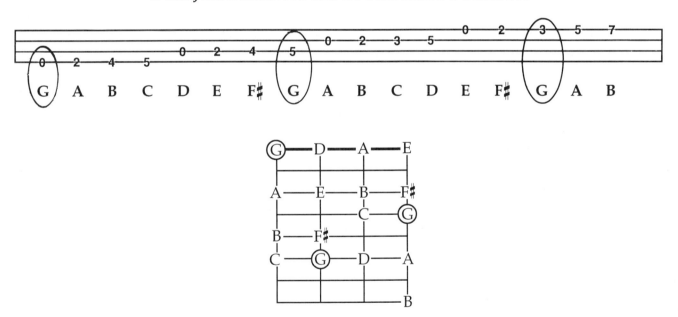

Except for rare minor or modal phrases and the "grace notes" produced by hammer-ons, pull-offs, and slides, these are the primary notes used to play most melodies in the key of G major. *Note:* in blues-oriented licks or when minor or modal chords such as the 7♭ and 3♭ chords are present, the palette can be expanded to include the flatted seventh and the flatted third tones of the major scale (the F natural and the B♭ notes in the key of G).

Just as in learning chords, the process of learning a melody by ear is one of trial-and-error. However, knowing the information and procedures in this book will reduce the guesswork immensely. The keys to playing by ear are to learn the rules and tendencies of musical composition, to listen very carefully, and to gain as much experience as possible. Most of the readers of this book already have the necessary listening skills - but many have not exercised those skills. The more you practice listening and guessing melody notes, the more proficient you will become at playing by ear. After much experience with the trial-and-error procedure, you will be playing by ear almost unconsciously. Now, the procedure:

LEARNING MELODIES BY EAR: THE TRIAL-AND-ERROR PROCEDURE

1) Learn the chord progression. Chapter 1 shows you how to do this by ear, or you can learn the chords from a songbook or ask other musicians. Write down the chords so you will have a basic road map.

2) Strum the key chord to give yourself a reference tone. Then strum the first chord of the song. It is usually the same as the key chord (**1** chord), but occasionally is the **4** chord.

3) Sing or hum *only* the first note. If working from a recording, stop the recording after the first note and sing or hum only that note.

4) Guess the identity of the note. Use your mandolin to sound the guessed note. Refer to your "palette" - the scale tones. There is a good chance that the melody note is one of the chord tones. Since there are only three notes in most of the chords you play, this narrows down the choices considerably. Hold the chord, playing the chord tones one at a time. Compare them to the note just sung to see if any of them are indeed the "mystery note". If not, proceed to the other four scale tones. Remember, if the 7♭ or 3♭ chord is present in the progression, the 3♭ or 7♭ notes should be added to the palette of possibilities.

5) Play the note you believe to be the correct note and ask yourself if it is *higher*, *lower*, or the *same* pitch as the note you sang or hummed. If it is the correct note, pat yourself on the back and proceed to the next note. If it is too high or too low in pitch, ask yourself *how much* too high or low it is, and select a note from the scale that is closer to the correct pitch.

6) Proceed note by note, until you have recreated an entire phrase. *Hint*- most phrases are either two or four measures in length. You may wish to write the phrase out in tablature or musical notation so you will not forget it.

7) Proceed to the next phrase, noting any chord changes. When you come to a chord change, strum the new chord first, then hum the "mystery note". Hearing the chord will help direct you to the proper pitch and give you a better overall impression of the phrase.

8) Listen for repetition. Listen not only to the individual notes but also to the phrases. Most songs have at least one melody phrase that occurs twice or even three times, repeating exactly or very closely. In an eight measure song part there are usually four two-measure phrases or two four-measure phrases. In a sixteen measure song part, look for four four-measure phrases or two eight-measure phrases. Sometimes as many as three phrases in a four-phrase song part may have the same or a similar melody line. In many songs, the melody of the entire chorus is exactly like that of the verse - only the lyrics and the presence or absence of vocal harmony are different. Often the first part of the verse and chorus are identical, but they end differently. If you learn to recognize repetition in the melody line, you can cut down your learning time by more than half in many songs.

9) Check your work. After you have finished, play along with the recording or live band from start to finish. If you find errors, rework the problem spots.

The trial-and-error procedure is demonstrated on the recording that accompanies this book using a sample song, *Boil Them Cabbage*. Listen to it carefully before proceeding. The resulting musical notation and tablature appear below.

Sample Song - Boil Them Cabbage

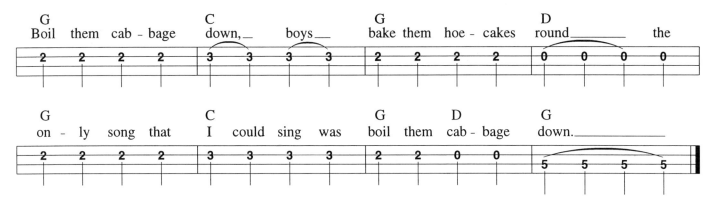

This is the essence of playing by ear. Though it may seem difficult at first, the trial-and-error procedure is absolutely necessary if you are going to truly learn this skill.

Learning Songs by Ear from Memory

Can you sing, hum, or whistle a song? If so, you know it well enough to begin learning it on your mandolin by ear. It would be best to re-create a few songs from memory first before actually learning by ear from a recording. Working strictly from memory eliminates the distraction of replaying bits of the recording over and over, while trying to hold the sound of a note in your mind. Simply choose a melody you can already sing or hum, but one that you do not already play on the mandolin. The quality of your singing is not important. If you must sing falsetto or with poor tone to produce the desired note, do not be concerned. If you are absolutely tone deaf, you can whistle the song. In fact, you can learn a song by merely *thinking* of the melody, but you will probably be more successful if you produce the sounds aloud.

The exercise on the following page will provide valuable practice in learning songs by ear from memory. This is probably the most important exercise in this book - it is your first effort at actually learning a melody by ear. Do not skip this exercise merely because you are uninterested in the choice of songs. Children's songs are chosen because they are known by all and because they tend to have simple, short melodies and frequent repetition of phrases.

Exercise 8

IDENTIFYING SIMPLE MELODIES FROM MEMORY

Use the trial-and-error procedure to learn the melodies of the following songs by ear. In case you do not know the melody of these popular children's songs, they are played for you on the demonstration recording (program number 22 on the recording). Listen to each melody until you have it memorized. You should be able to sing or whistle it without referring to written music. Using the trial-and-error procedure, find the correct melody notes on your mandolin. Write in the melodies below, using an erasable pencil. It is not absolutely necessary to include timing stems, though your melody notes should appear in the proper segments of the proper measure. Chords are provided. *Answers can be found on page 88.*

Mary Had a Little Lamb

G	G	D	G

G	G	D	G

Skip to My Lou

G	G	D	D

G	G	D	G

This Old Man (Knick-Knack, Paddy-Whack)

G	G	G	D

G	G	G	D G

Learning Songs by Ear from Recordings

The preceding exercise should have familiarized you with the trial-and-error procedure. We will now begin to learn unfamiliar songs by ear, using a recording as a source. However, we must first clarify some aspects of song arrangements that may cause confusion when learning an unfamiliar song from a recording.

Instrumental Introductions and Solos

As mentioned earlier, vocal songs often start with an instrumental introduction consisting of a full or partial solo. Common intros coincide with a **1 - 5 - 1 - 1** or a **5 - 5 - 1 - 1** chord sequence. The intro is often exactly the same in melody and chord structure as the last four measures of the verse or chorus. Solos can be short phrases like four-bar turnarounds, especially in gospel music, but are more often an entire song part in country and bluegrass music.

Disregard instrumental intros and solos for now. Learn the melody strictly from the vocal part. Soloists usually take liberties with the melody - few solos are completely accurate, and most are much more complex than the vocal melody. Learning instrumental parts by ear is something that will come much easier after experience with vocal melodies.

More About Pickup Notes

Unlike the children's songs you worked out in Exercise 8, most songs do not start neatly on the first beat of the measure. In order to locate the first beat of the first full measure so we will have a viable starting point, we must learn to identify and count *pickup notes*. As mentioned in Chapter 1, pickup notes occur at the very beginning of the song, before the chord progression starts. They will almost always occupy less than a full measure. The pickup notes are sometimes actual melody notes that are sung by the vocalist. We will call these *melody pickups*. In the song *Will the Circle Be Unbroken*, the notes that occur on the first two words are melody pickups. If you listen to a band performing this song, you will notice that the music has a noticeable pulse or swell on the first syllable of the word **"cir**-cle", and every four beats after that. This pulse coincides with the first beat of each measure. All the chord changes in this song occur on the first beat of a measure. Count along (**"One**, two, three, four; **One**, two, three, four..." *etc.*) to get the feel of where the first beat of each measure is. When a song repeats, notice on what counts the pickup notes occur. In the following example, they occur on the beats of three and four.

Note - In this book, all melody notes are in boldface type

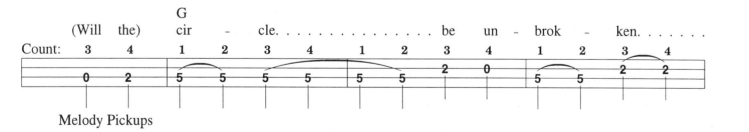

Melody Pickups

Often the first melody note does not occur until the first beat of the first complete measure, but instrumental pickup notes are played prior to this. We will call these *non-melody pickups.* They are used to signal to the rhythm instruments when to begin and simply to fill up space between song parts. Remember, the last partial measure of a song and the pickups should equal a complete measure, with all beats accounted for. Non-melody pickups are fairly easy to discern in a vocal song - though there will be a note or notes played by an instrumentalist, no words will coincide. The following first line of *Two Dollar Bill* is an example. Note the three instrumental pickup notes that "lead" up the scale to the first melody note that is actually sung by the vocalist. *(Melody notes boldfaced.)*

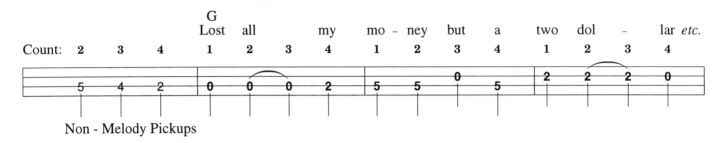

Non - Melody Pickups

Sometimes the first word or two of the lyrics occur during the pickup measure, but there is also a pickup note (or notes) played by an instrumentalist prior to these melody pickups. In other words, the pickup measure contains melody pickups *and* non-melody pickups. The first line of the song *Mountain Dew* as arranged below is an example.

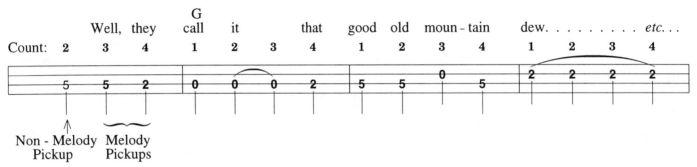

Non - Melody   Melody
Pickup   Pickups

There is no standard number of pickup notes. Remember, though, the last partial measure of the song plus the pickups must equal a full measure - four beats in 4/4 time or 3 beats in 3/4 time. All beats must be accounted for, whether by notes or rests. Remember also that the starting point of the rhythm instruments marks the first beat of the first complete measure. Any notes played and/or sung prior to this are pickup notes.

Locating First-beat Melody Notes

It is very difficult to begin by trying to figure out every single melody note in a song. However, if you can identify only the notes that fall on the all-important first beat of the measure, you will have a basic arrangement that can be recognized. You can later modify this arrangement, adding other melody notes as you become more familiar with the song. To locate first-beat melody notes when working from a recording:

Start the recording, stopping it immediately after the first note. Identify this note using the trial-and-error procedure. Remember, if the first note does not occur on the first beat of the measure, it is a pickup note. Continue through the song, identifying any pickups and all first-beat melody notes. Write them down on the blank staves provided. Be sure to place all first-beat melody notes just to the right of the measure lines to allow room for other notes to be added in later exercises.

The trial-and-error procedure is demonstrated on the tape using the sample song, *Worried Man Blues*. Below is the resulting first-beat melody arrangement.

Worried Man Blues - First-beat Melody Notes

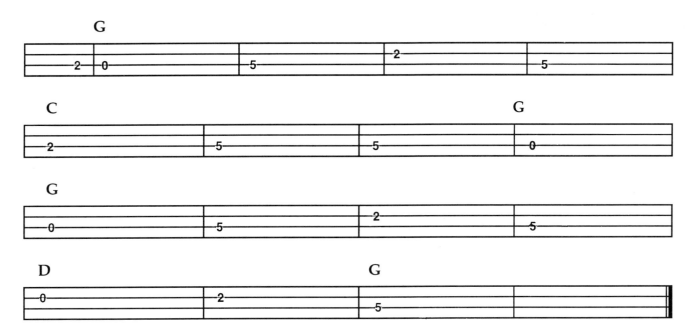

Exercise 9

LOCATING FIRST-BEAT MELODY NOTES

With the balance control of your stereo in the middle position, listen to Song Example # 1 (program number 24 on the recording). Using the trial-and-error procedure outlined on page 32, identify all first-beat melody notes. Write them in tablature on the blank staves below. Be sure to use an erasable pencil, for you will be modifying your arrangement in subsequent exercises. *The answer arrangement appears on page 89.*

Song Example # 1 - First-beat Melody Notes

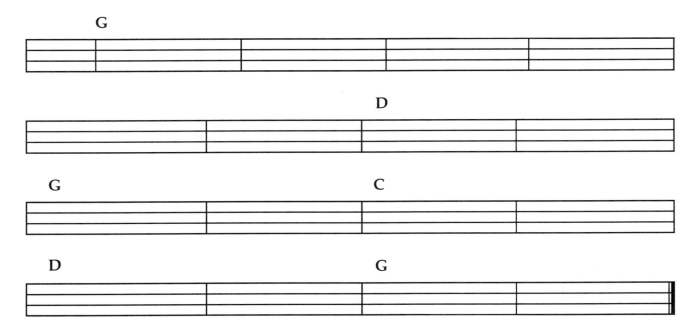

Using Fill Licks

This arrangement is very simplistic. The notes are so far apart it probably sounds boring to you. We can remedy this by "filling in" the spaces with a simple lick. A *lick* is a short musical phrase that can be inserted in specific chord situations. Consider licks to be musical building blocks. Play the following fill lick with a *bum-di-dy, bum, bum* rhythm. Use a *down, down-up, down, down* pick motion: (the symbol ⊓ means downstroke, the symbol ∧ means upstroke)

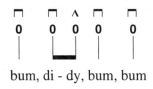

bum, di - dy, bum, bum

To incorporate the fill lick into your first-beat melody arrangement, note the first-beat melody notes with the left hand and play the rhythmic fill pattern on the same string with the right hand. The following is the first-beat arrangement of the sample song, *Worried Man Blues*, first-beat melody notes, with fill licks added. Melody notes are boldfaced. Be sure to emphasize these notes when playing the arrangement.

Worried Man Blues - First-beat Melody Notes with Fill Licks

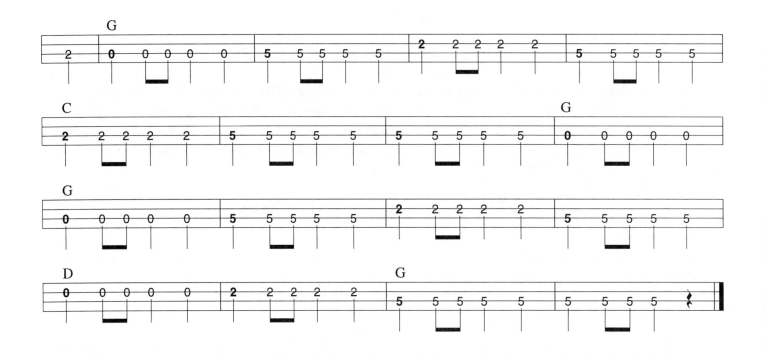

Exercise 10

USING FILL LICKS

Modify the first-beat melody arrangement you created for Song Example #1 on the previous page, adding fill licks to create a fuller sounding, more interesting solo. *The answer arrangement appears on page 89.*

Using Phrasing Licks

When writing, we use commas to separate phrases. We use periods to signal the end of sentences. Just as we talk and write in phrases, we also play music in phrases. The preceding arrangement was very monotonous - not only was the same lick repeated over and over, but there was no phrasing - it was like a speech that had been typed with no commas or periods. In music, there are specific licks that serve as musical commas and periods.

Lead-ins

The *lead-in* is a lick that has a dual purpose. It can serve as a "comma" to separate musical phrases, and it leads the ear up or down the scale to the upcoming melody note. Lead-ins are essentially the same as pickup notes, except that they occur within the song, whereas pickups occur at the beginning of the song. Lead-ins can consume the whole measure or as little as one beat. To construct an ascending lead-in, simply play the scale tones that precede the upcoming melody note, as shown in the example below. The G major scale is reproduced below so you can see the adjacent scale tones

THE G MAJOR SCALE

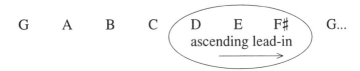

UPCOMING MELODY NOTE (G)

ASCENDING LEAD-IN

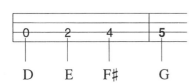

To construct a descending lead-in, play the *succeeding* scale tones in reverse order:

UPCOMING MELODY NOTE (G)

DESCENDING LEAD-IN

The upcoming melody note dictates which lead-in notes are valid. You may also want to relate your lead-in to the previous melody note. If the upcoming melody note is higher in pitch than the one just played, it would make sense to use an ascending lead-in. If the upcoming melody note is lower in pitch than the previous melody note, you could play scale tones in reverse order to form a descending lead-in:

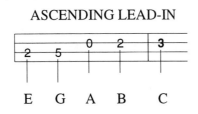

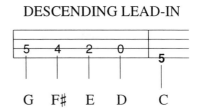

If there are not enough major scale tones between the former melody note and the upcoming melody note to fill up the measure, *chromatics* (notes in between the scale tones) can be used, or a note can be repeated as many times as necessary:

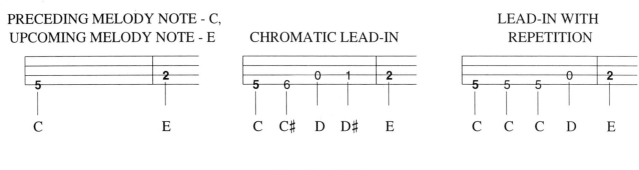

The Tag Lick

The *tag lick* is the "period" at the end of a musical "sentence". It is used where an actual period is called for in the lyrics or where a fill-in of longer than one measure is required. It always occurs at the end of a phrase or song part, and therefore is based on the key (1) note.

The tag lick occupies five beats, leaving an incomplete measure. This partial measure can be occupied by a fill lick or by a lead-in to the upcoming melody note:

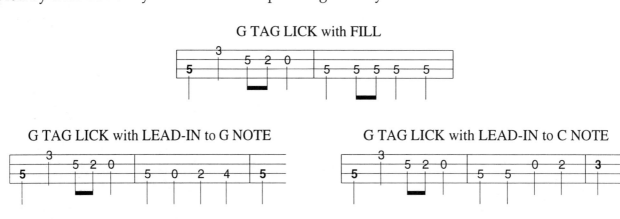

The following arrangement of *Worried Man Blues* includes lead-ins acting as musical "commas" between phrases, and a tag lick at the end to serve as a musical "period".

Worried Man Blues - Phrasing Licks Added

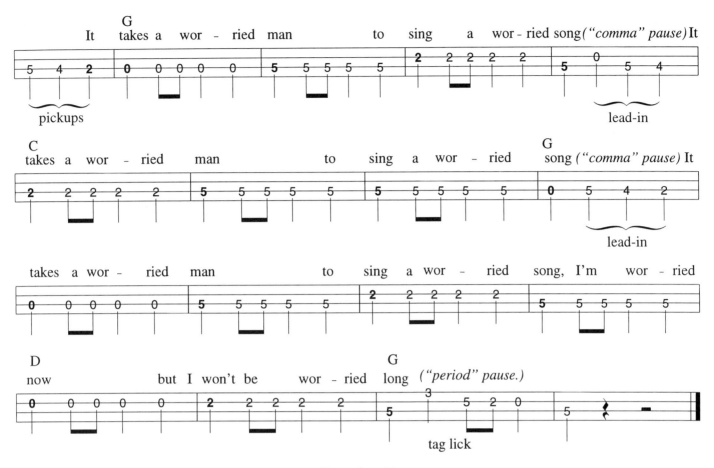

Exercise 11

USING PHRASING LICKS

Again modify the arrangement you created for Song Example #1 (page 37) adding phrasing licks in appropriate locations. Use the blank staves below to write out your revised arrangement. Use an erasable pencil, as you will be modifying this arrangement again later. *Although there is no one correct answer, a sample answer appears on page 90.*

Song Example # 1 - First-beat Melody Notes with Phrasing Licks

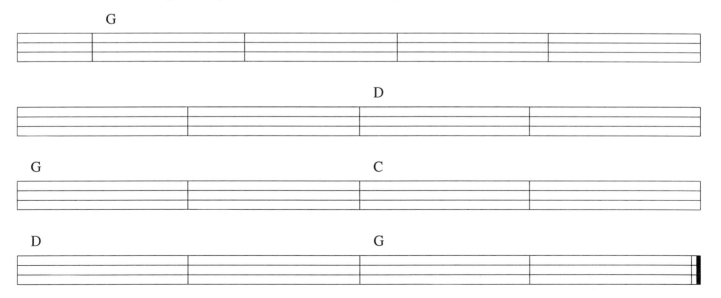

Identifying Last-beat Melody Notes

Though the first beat of the measure is the location of the most important melody notes, many crucial melody notes also occur on the last beat of the measure. If you can play most of the melody notes that occur on the first *and* last beats of each measure, the resulting solo will be very true to the melody. The last-beat melody notes can be identified by the trial-and-error procedure - then the last note of the fill lick can be changed to the proper note. The first measure of *Worried Man Blues* is used below as an example:

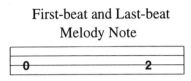

First-beat and Last-beat
Melody Note

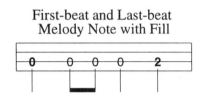

First-beat and Last-beat
Melody Note with Fill

At times the melody note that occurs on the first beat is held throughout the measure, with no new melody note on the last beat, or there is a melody note, but it is the same as the first-beat melody note. In this situation merely play the fill lick unaltered. Measure thirteen of *Worried Man Blues* is an example:

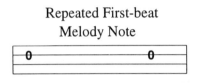

Repeated First-beat
Melody Note

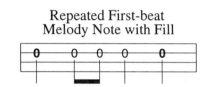

Repeated First-beat
Melody Note with Fill

The sample song *Worried Man Blues* is presented below as a first-beat and last-beat melody arrangement. On the following page, the melody oriented solo (page 41) is modified to include the last-beat melody notes (melody notes boldfaced).

Worried Man Blues - First-beat and Last-beat Melody Notes

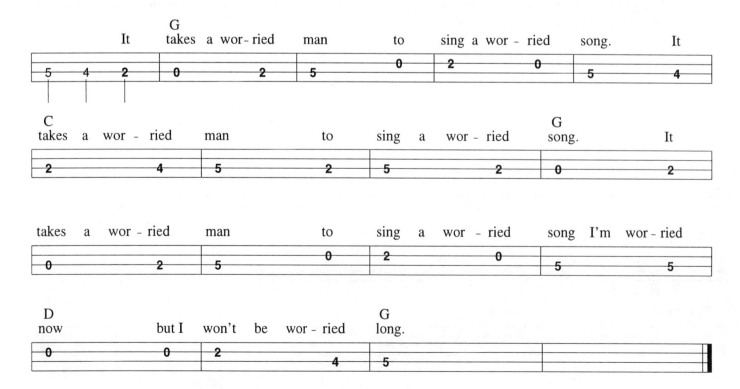

Worried Man Blues - First-beat and Last-beat Melody Oriented Solo

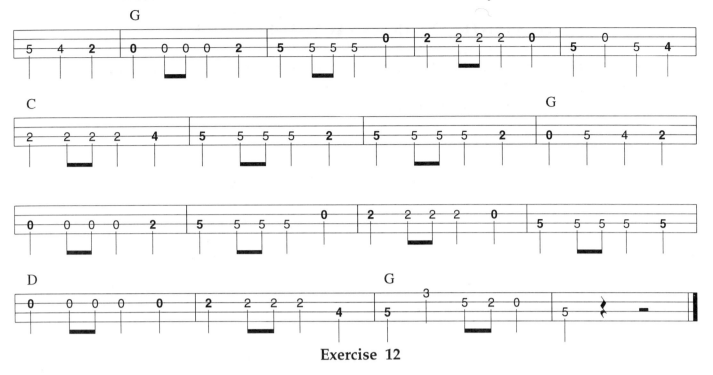

Exercise 12

CREATING A FIRST-BEAT AND LAST-BEAT MELODY ORIENTED ARRANGEMENT

Listen again to Song Example # 1 on the demonstration recording (program number 25). Identify the melody note that occurs on the last beat of each measure. Modify your previous arrangement (page 41) to include all last-beat melody notes. *Answer arrangement appears on page 90.*

Locating Internal Melody Notes

Passages in many songs will include important melody notes in between the first and last beats of the measure. Use the trial-and-error procedure to identify the internal melody notes, then alter the fill lick to include these notes. Compare the first-beat and last-beat arrangement of *Worried Man Blues* above to the following arrangement to see how the internal melody notes were incorporated (melody notes boldfaced).

Worried Man Blues - All Melody Notes with Phrasing Licks

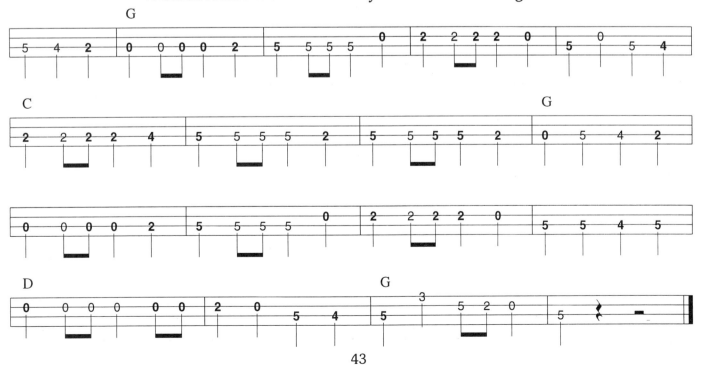

Exercise 13

IDENTIFYING INTERNAL MELODY NOTES

Alter your first-beat and last-beat melody-oriented arrangement of Song Example #1 (page 41) to include all internal melody notes. *Due to the multiple choice of licks, there is no one correct answer. However, a sample answer arrangement appears on page 91.*

Exercise 14

CREATING A MELODY ARRANGEMENT BY EAR "FROM SCRATCH"

Listen to Song Example # 2 on the demonstration recording (program number 24). Create a melody-oriented solo for this song, complete with fill licks and phrasing licks. Write out your arrangement below. *Although there is no one correct answer, a sample answer appears on page 91.*

Song Example #2

verse: G

D   G

D   G

chorus:
C   G

C   G   D

G

D   G

Creating Melody-Oriented Solos in 3/4 Time

To create melody oriented solos in 3/4 time, the principles are the same as described in the preceding pages, except that four beat licks will be shortened to three beats by omitting a note. Below is a fill lick and some sample phrasing licks in 3/4 time, key of G.

FILL LICK in 3/4 TIME

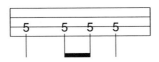

Since 3/4 time songs are played at slow tempos, the tremolo will often be employed whenever a melody note lasts longer than one beat. The tablature symbol for tremolo is a diagonal line on the note stem. Simply play the note with a "fanning" motion, striking the string with the pick several times per second. Perform the fanning motion for the duration of beats indicated. For example, if two adjacent quarter notes have the diagonal line, fan the note consistently for two beats. The key to a good tremolo is not so much the speed of the fanning as it is keeping an equal amount of time between strikes of the pick. Tilting the pick slightly so that it strikes the strings at an angle will help you perform a smooth tremolo.

TREMOLO

Lead-ins are also the same in 3/4 time, only they will last no longer than three beats:

LEAD-IN: G to C NOTE

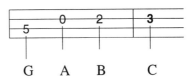

LEAD-IN: C or D to G NOTE

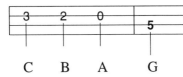

LEAD-IN: C to D NOTE

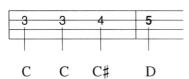

The tag lick can also be shortened to fit into a three-beat measure:

TAG LICK, 3/4 TIME

TAG LICK, 3/4 TIME with FILL

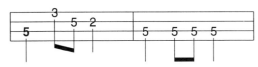

TAG LICK with LEAD-IN to G NOTE

TAG LICK with LEAD-IN to C NOTE

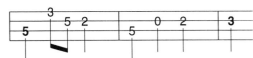

Below is the basic melody of *Amazing Grace*. Following that is an arrangement of the same song demonstrating the use of fill licks and phrasing licks to create a melody-oriented solo in 3/4 time.

Amazing Grace - Basic Melody

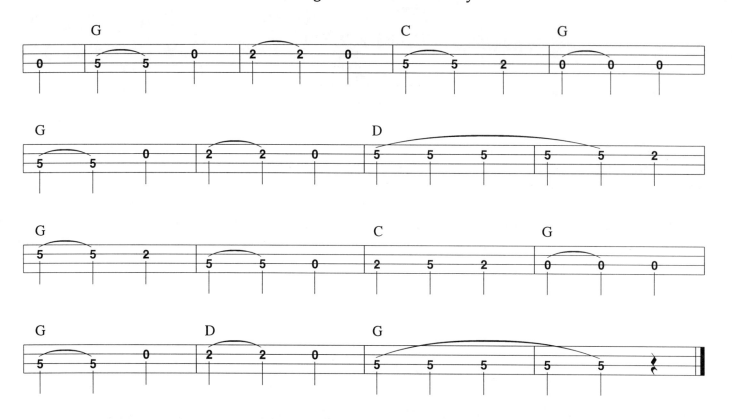

Amazing Grace - Melody Oriented Solo with Phrasing Licks in 3/4 Time

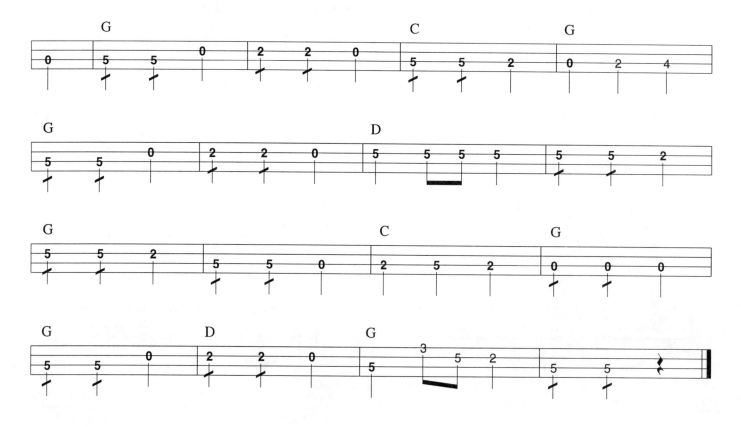

CREATING A MELODY ORIENTED SOLO IN 3/4 TIME

Listen to Song Example #3, which is in 3/4 time. Learn the melody by ear and write it on the first set of blank staves below. Then combine the melody with fill licks, tremolo, and phrasing licks. Write out your melody oriented solo on the second set of blank staves. *Although there is no one correct answer, a sample answer appears on page 92.*

Song Example # 3 - Melody

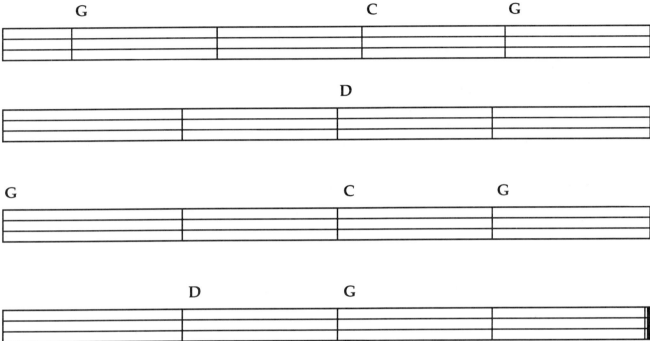

Song Example # 3 - Melody Oriented Solo with Phrasing Licks

Learning Quickly-Changing Melodies by Ear

An acceptable melody-oriented solo can be arranged for most songs by playing the melody notes that occur on the first and last beats of the measure and inserting fill licks and phrasing licks at the appropriate places. You can also locate and identify passages that contain internal melody notes which are essential for an accurate rendition. But in some songs there are important internal melody notes throughout the song. In these songs, it will be necessary to carry the trial-and-error procedure a step further, applying it to virtually every beat in the song. It is easy enough to determine which songs require further trial-and-error treatment: If you identify the melody notes that occur on the first and last beats, but your arrangement is still not accurate enough that listeners can identify the song, you are probably dealing with a quickly-changing melody that will need more revision.

Notice the lyrics of the sample song *Cripple Creek* below. There are melody notes on almost every beat. That means that, after we have performed the trial-and-error procedure on all beats within every measure, the resulting basic melody arrangement will be the final product - there is no room for fill licks. In this particular song, there are not even enough beats at the end of song parts to insert tag licks. The melody fills up all the available space in the song except for the last beat of every other measure. This brief pause is what punctuates the song. These one-beat pauses in the melody divide the entire song into two-measure phrases - the pauses do the job of the phrasing licks.

Note that in *Cripple Creek*, we carried the trial-and-error procedure as far as possible, identifying even the melody notes that occur on the second half of certain beats. Every syllable of the lyrics is duplicated in the instrumental version. This results in the use of eighth notes in our instrumental arrangement. Not only does this produce a thoroughly accurate arrangement with no melody notes omitted, but the occasional eighth note passages create much-needed rhythmic variation. A song composed entirely of quarter notes would be very monotonous.

Cripple Creek - Basic Melody/Melody - Oriented Solo

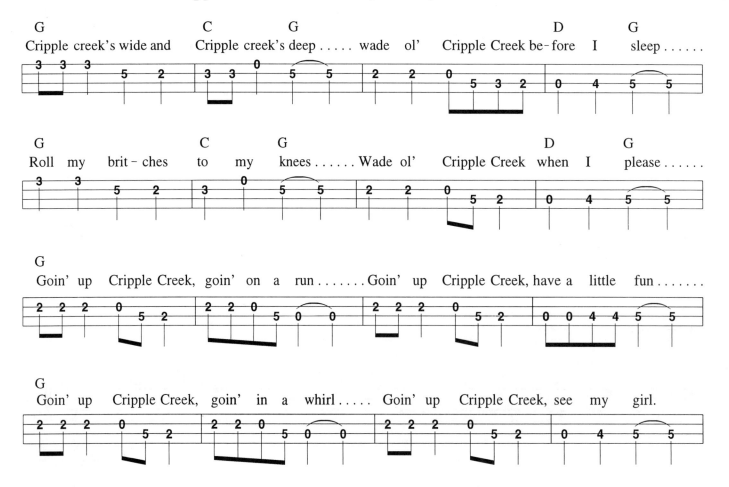

Exercise 16a

LEARNING QUICKLY-CHANGING MELODIES BY EAR

Listen to Song Example #4, a quickly-changing melody. Learn the melody by ear and write your melody oriented solo below. *A sample answer appears on page 93.*

Song Example # 4 - Melody-Oriented Solo

verse
G   G   D

G   D   G

chorus
G   D   G

G   D   G

Exercise 16b

Listen to Song Example #5, a quickly-changing melody. Learn the melody and write your melody oriented solo below. *A sample answer appears on page 93.*

Song Example #5 - Melody-Oriented Solo

verse
G   G   C   G   G   D

G   G   C   G   D   G

chorus (instrumental)
G   D   G

G   D   G

Exercise 16c

Listen to Song Example # 6, a quickly-changing melody in 3/4 time. Learn the melody by ear and write your melody oriented solo below. *A sample answer appears on page 94.*

Song Example # 6

```
        G        C    G                      D    G
  |-------------|-------------|-------------|-------------|-------------|
  |-------------|-------------|-------------|-------------|-------------|
  |-------------|-------------|-------------|-------------|-------------|
  |-------------|-------------|-------------|-------------|-------------|
```

```
  D                    G             D             G
  |-------------------|-------------|-------------|-------------|
  |-------------------|-------------|-------------|-------------|
  |-------------------|-------------|-------------|-------------|
  |-------------------|-------------|-------------|-------------|
```

```
  G              C    G                    D     G
  |-------------|-------------|-------------|-------------||
  |-------------|-------------|-------------|-------------||
  |-------------|-------------|-------------|-------------||
  |-------------|-------------|-------------|-------------||
```

Use the following blank staves to experiment or take notes.

```
  |-------------|-------------|-------------|-------------|
  |-------------|-------------|-------------|-------------|
  |-------------|-------------|-------------|-------------|
  |-------------|-------------|-------------|-------------|
```

```
  |-------------|-------------|-------------|-------------|
  |-------------|-------------|-------------|-------------|
  |-------------|-------------|-------------|-------------|
  |-------------|-------------|-------------|-------------|
```

```
  |-------------|-------------|-------------|-------------|
  |-------------|-------------|-------------|-------------|
  |-------------|-------------|-------------|-------------|
  |-------------|-------------|-------------|-------------|
```

```
  |-------------|-------------|-------------|-------------|
  |-------------|-------------|-------------|-------------|
  |-------------|-------------|-------------|-------------|
  |-------------|-------------|-------------|-------------|
```

```
  |-------------|-------------|-------------|-------------|
  |-------------|-------------|-------------|-------------|
  |-------------|-------------|-------------|-------------|
  |-------------|-------------|-------------|-------------|
```

```
  |-------------|-------------|-------------|-------------|
  |-------------|-------------|-------------|-------------|
  |-------------|-------------|-------------|-------------|
  |-------------|-------------|-------------|-------------|
```

```
  |-------------|-------------|-------------|-------------|
  |-------------|-------------|-------------|-------------|
  |-------------|-------------|-------------|-------------|
  |-------------|-------------|-------------|-------------|
```

Chapter 3

USING LICKS

If you have worked through the step-by-step procedures presented in this book and applied the principles to new songs, you should now have a pretty good foundation in learning songs on the mandolin by ear. Be proud of yourself - being able to reproduce an accurate melody by ear is no small accomplishment.

But what about licks? You have no doubt heard accomplished mandolinists play passages which sound really flashy and show technical skill, but may not bear any resemblance to the melody. You probably already play many of these licks yourself as part of memorized solos, but you may not know how to use them at will.

In a vocal song, the singer sings the melody. The tasteful instrumental soloist will play an initial solo that is very close to the melody line, especially if it is an introductory solo. Most songs include at least three verses and choruses and at least two instrumental solos. Even with beautiful singing and perfect instrumental execution, the same melody line repeated ten times in succession may become monotonous. For this reason, the instrumentalist often inserts interesting phrases that bear little or no resemblance to the melody. Later in the song, after the melody has been well-established, he may play an entire solo that is not melody oriented, but simply sounds good - one that shows off his skill and the uniqueness of his instrument. The content of this solo is limited only by the meter and chord progression. The term for this is *improvising*.

You may ask "What is the difference between improvising and faking?" A faked solo really is improvising, but it occurs because the player does not know how to play the melody. We will define an improvised solo as one in which the soloist intentionally departs from the melody to make the song more interesting. How would a listener know whether you are improvising or faking? He probably wound not be able to tell the difference - but *you* would. If you want to experience the thrill of spontaneously creating original arrangements and turning some heads in a jam session, spend some time experimenting with the ideas in this chapter.

The *lick* is the building block of the improvised solo. A lick is a phrase that stands on its own as a musical idea. Licks can be interchanged and combined according to the tastes and ability of the individual player. Every accomplished mandolinist has "signature licks" that he has created himself or adapted from the playing of others. Some original licks are meticulously worked out to fit a certain chord or melody situation. Sometimes licks originate as "happy mistakes"- phrases that were not planned, but sounded good enough for the player to remember and add to his bag of tricks. Most licks are learned from recordings, books, videos, or the old-fashioned way - from other players.

Most mandolinists learn songs by rote - they either copy another player or use written music. Their arrangements are usually "carved in stone" - they are performed exactly the same every time. There is nothing wrong with this - even the best mandolinists often play pre-planned arrangements when performing. But for inexperienced players, one missed note can lead to a "wreck" which cannot be recovered from without breaking time. When playing memorized arrangements each note is linked to the adjacent one. When a note is missed, it is like breaking a link in a chain - the whole thing becomes non-functional. One important aspect of learning to view licks as interchangeable components is the enhanced ability to recover from mistakes without breaking time. Experienced players can insert a familiar lick that fits the chord and allows them to return to the intended arrangement without a timing lapse. Listeners are never aware of the mistake.

The tasteful musician will play according to the guidelines of the situation. When playing in a band, the main idea is to support the vocals. The ability to reproduce the melody, "chop" rhythm, and play tasteful backup is essential. In a jam session, the rules are less strict. If you are arranging a solo to be used in a band or contest situation, melody playing and strategically placed hot licks both go into producing an acceptable arrangement.

Do not misunderstand - the use of licks does not preclude playing the melody. Licks can be used to render accurate melodies. We will learn more about that later in this chapter.

Faking With Licks

You used the fill licks and phrasing licks in Chapter 2 as building blocks to create a solo. You can use the licks presented in this chapter the same way to "fake" a solo based only on the chord progression. Simply insert an appropriate lick into a given chord situation. For example, for any measure of G chord, insert a G lick. For any measure of C chord, insert a C lick, and so on. Though most licks can be used almost anywhere in the arrangement that the chord progression allows, the tag licks should only be used at the end of phrases and song parts. Otherwise, the solo may not make sense - the "period" at the end of musical sentences may not be obvious, or may appear awkwardly in the middle of phrases.

The licks that follow are designed to be moved around the fingerboard so they can be used in many different chord situations. There are only fifteen different patterns. Once you learn the 'G' licks, you have already learned the 'C' and 'D' licks - it is simply a matter of moving the 'G' fingerboard pattern to a different fingerboard location. 'G' lick #1, 'C' lick #1, and "D" lick #1 are the same pattern. 'G' lick #2, 'C' lick #2, and "D" lick #2 are the same pattern, and so on.

After a pattern is moved from one chord situation to another, some notes may be more easily played on a different string and/or fret than in the original lick. Using the easier fingering changes the "shape" of the lick, but the sound of the lick remains the same. In the lists that follow, the original fingering of the note is in parentheses and the "easier" fingering is on the same note stem, but without parentheses. In the sample arrangements, the easier fingering is used. *Tip* - Licks # 1, 5, 6, 10 and 11 are based on the popular bluegrass major chord formation. Start out with this chord formation in place, and the left hand fingering will be obvious, many notes already in place or easily reached.

Occasionally in moving a pattern to a different chord situation, a note or two may be shifted out of the desired key. Often this sounds fine - flatted thirds and sevenths are examples. But if a note sounds too harsh, simply move it up or down one fret to the proper scale tone.

Many of these licks sound "unfinished" because they do not end on a chord root. The phrasing licks you insert at the end of musical phrases and song parts will supply the necessary "commas" and "periods" so the arrangement will make sense compositionally. Two new tag licks are included to add variety to your arrangements.

When inserting these licks, repetition is important for a tasteful arrangement. Use the same lick in different chord situations. For example, if you use G lick # 1 followed by G lick #4, then the chord changes to **C**, use C lick #1 followed by C lick #4. This kind of repetition imposes order into what would otherwise be a random assortment of licks. Also use repetition of entire phrases. If you use a ceretain sequence of licks for a certain melody or lyrical phrase, and the same phrase appears later in the song part, repeat the previous lick sequence also. Not only will the use of repetition create a more tasteful arrangement, but the arrangement will be easier to learn. In an eight-bar song part, you may not be required to use more than three or four lick patterns!

G LICKS

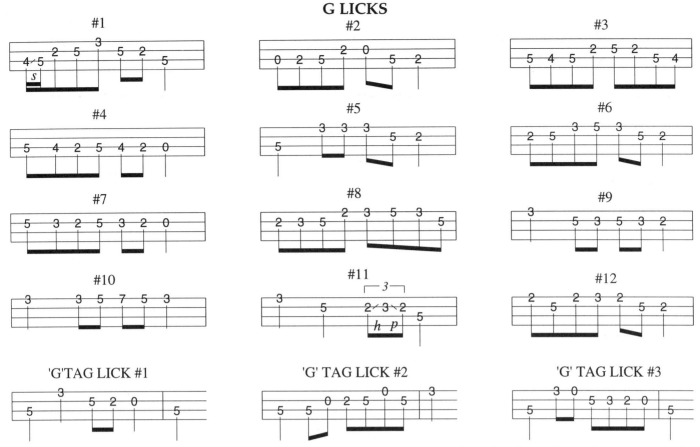

Below is the previous arrangement of *Worried Man Blues* (page 43) with selected G licks inserted. This arrangement can be heard on the demonstration recording.

Worried Man Blues - G Licks Inserted

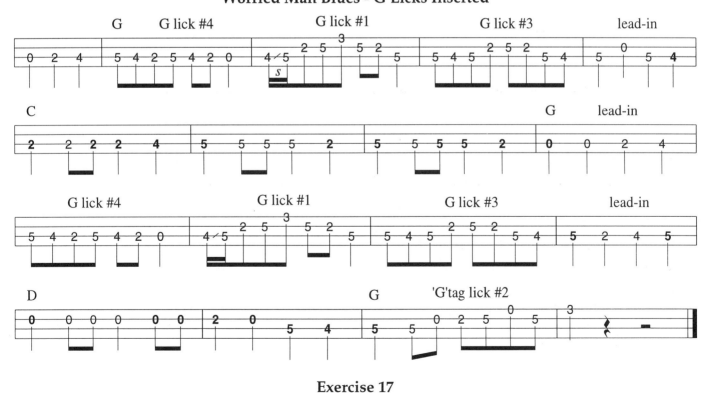

Exercise 17

INSERTING G LICKS

Return to the arrangements that you created earlier for Song Examples # 1, 2, 4 and 5. Insert G licks from the previous list in appropriate places. You may write out your revised arrangement using the blank staves found at the end of this chapter. *Because of the many choices and possibilities, there is no answer arrangement presented.*

C LICKS

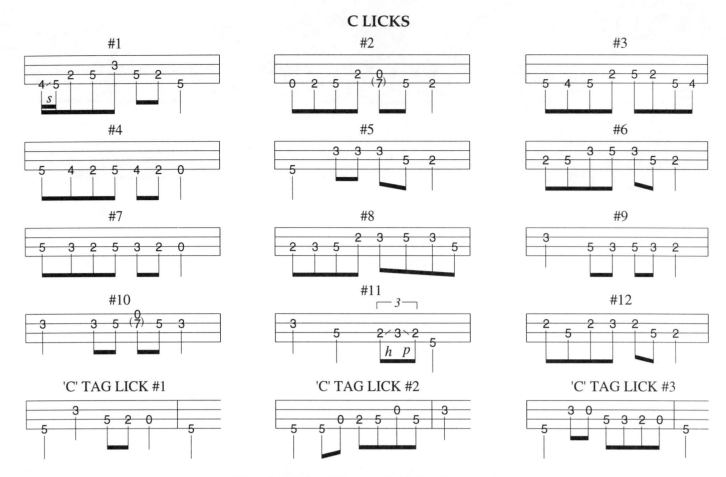

Worried Man Blues - C Licks Inserted

This arrangement can be heard on the demonstration recording.

Exercise 18
INSERTING C LICKS

Return to the arrangements that you created earlier for Song Examples # 1, 2, 4, and 5. Insert C licks from the preceding list in appropriate places. You may wish to write out your revised arrangement using the blank staves found at the end of this chapter. *Because of the many choices and possibilities, there is no answer arrangement presented.*

D LICKS

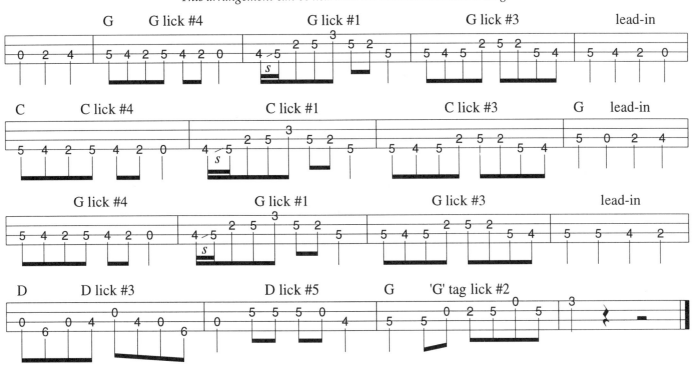

Worried Man Blues - D Licks Inserted

This arrangement can be heard on the demonstration recording.

Exercise 19
INSERTING D LICKS

Return to the arrangements that you created earlier for Song Examples # 1, 2, 4, and 5. Insert D licks from the preceding list in appropriate places. You may wish to write out your revised arrangement using the blank staves found at the end of this chapter. *Because of the many choices and possibilities, there is no answer arrangement presented.*

Creating a Melody Oriented Solo Using Licks

Learning to fake a solo by inserting licks is a valuable skill which can increase your creativity and your ability to jam with others. But there is yet another level. Remember, *faking* is what you do when you cannot yet play the melody. Playing strictly from licks, though a valuable skill, can eventually become a dead end. If your repitiore of licks is limited, all of your solos may sound alike. On the other hand, if you develop a large repitiore of licks but use them indiscriminately, your solos will often be in poor taste. That is why we learned how to render a melody before attempting to improvise with licks.

We will now learn how to play recognizable melody-oriented solos using licks. You can select licks that allow you to render any melody you may encounter. Remember, the first-beat melody note is the most important. To render a melody using licks, simply choose a lick that is associated with the proper chord, and whose first note is the same as the first-beat melody note. The first measure of *Worried Man Blues* is used below for demonstration (see melody arrangement, page 37). The melody notes are boldfaced.

If you do not know an acceptable lick that begins with the correct melody note, you can alter a lick, changing the first note to the correct melody note. The second measure of *Worried Man Blues* (page 37) is used below to demonstrate:

Worried Man Blues - First-beat Melody Oriented Solo Using Licks
This arrangement can be heard on the demonstration recording.

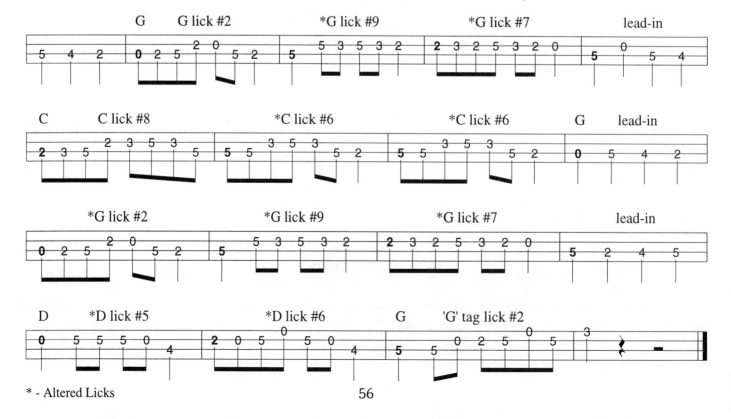

* - Altered Licks

Including Last-beat Melody Notes

For a more recognizable rendition, you may wish to also include the last-beat melody notes in your arrangement. Simply choose a lick that allows access not only to the first-beat melody note, but also the last-beat melody note. The first measure of *Worried Man Blues* again serves as an example (see first-beat and last-beat melody arrangement, page 42). In the sample arrangement, G lick # 2 was chosen because it contains the correct melody notes on the first and last beats of the measure:

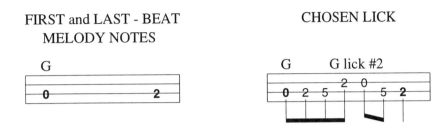

Again, if the chosen lick does not contain the proper melody note on the last beat of the measure, either choose a lick that does or choose a lick that can be easily altered to include the correct melody note.

Below is the previous arrangement of the sample song *Worried Man Blues* (page 56) with selected licks altered to allow the sounding of the first-beat and last-beat melody notes. The first-beat and last-beat melody notes are in boldface type. Be sure to emphasize the melody notes as you play any melody oriented arrangement.

Worried Man Blues - First-beat and Last-beat Melody Oriented Solo Using Licks

This arrangement can be heard on the demonstration recording.

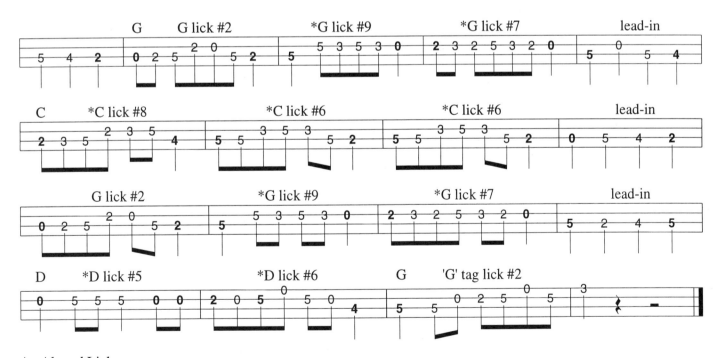

* - Altered Licks

Including Internal Melody Notes

Measures 12 through 14 of *Worried Man Blues* contain internal melody notes on almost every beat. In this situation, playing the melody as sung will usually be satisfactory:

INTERNAL MELODY NOTES, AS SUNG:

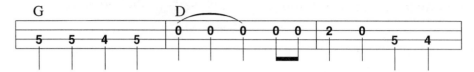

. . .or, you may wish to let the situation dictate an original lick by merely filling in eighth notes around the existing melody notes:

INTERNAL MELODY NOTES, FILL NOTES AROUND MELODY

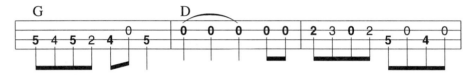

If you do happen to know a lick that already contains the correct melody notes or can be easily altered to include them, you may choose to use it:

INTERNAL MELODY NOTES INCLUDED IN LICKS

The following arrangement of *Worried Man Blues* uses licks throughout, and includes all internal melody notes (melody notes boldfaced).

Worried Man Blues, Using Licks - Internal Melody Notes Included
This arrangement can be heard on the demonstration recording.

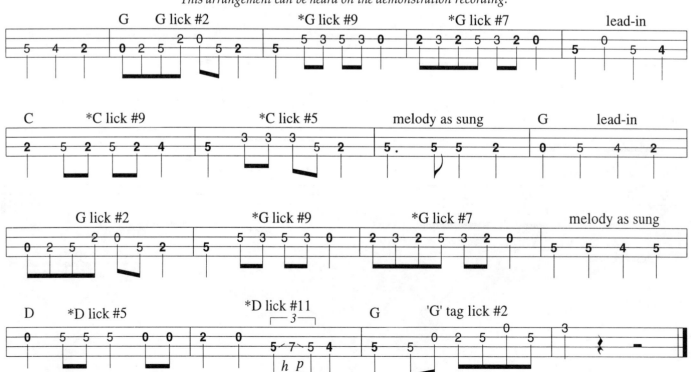

* - Altered Licks

58

USING LICKS TO CREATE A MELODY ORIENTED SOLO BY EAR

Return to the arrangements that you created earlier for Song Examples # 1, 2, 4, and 5. Either alter existing licks to include melody notes, or select new licks that will best allow access to important melody notes. Remember, it is not necessary to sound every melody note, though you should try to sound at least the first melody note of each measure or phrase. You may use the blank staves at the end of this chapter to record your arrangements. *Because of the many possibilities, there is no answer arrangement presented.*

Using Hot Licks

It is up to you whether to stick to an accurate melody arrangement or to throw in a few hot licks for "show". As mentioned earlier, an introductory solo should be fairly close to the melody as sung. If your solo occurs later in the song after the melody is well established, you may be more creative. If you do choose to "show off", the most effective place to use a hot lick is at the end of your solo. Most song parts end with either a **5 - 5 - 1 -1** or a **1 - 5 - 1 - 1** chord sequence. In the key of G, this is a **D - D - G - G** or a **G - D - G - G** sequence. Below are some hot licks that fit these situations.

HOT LICK #1

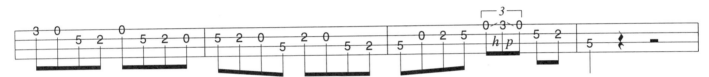

HOT LICK #2
Flatted thirds and sevenths are used to create a bluesy sound.

HOT LICK #3
Triplets are used in this lick (a triplet is a group of three notes played in one beat)

HOT LICK #4
Flatted thirds and sevenths *and* triplets are used in this lick.

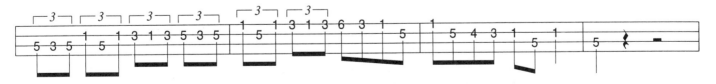

The following arrangement of *Worried Man Blues* is the previous arrangement (page 58) with a hot lick added at the end.

Worried Man Blues, with Hot Lick

This arrangement can be heard on the demonstration recording.

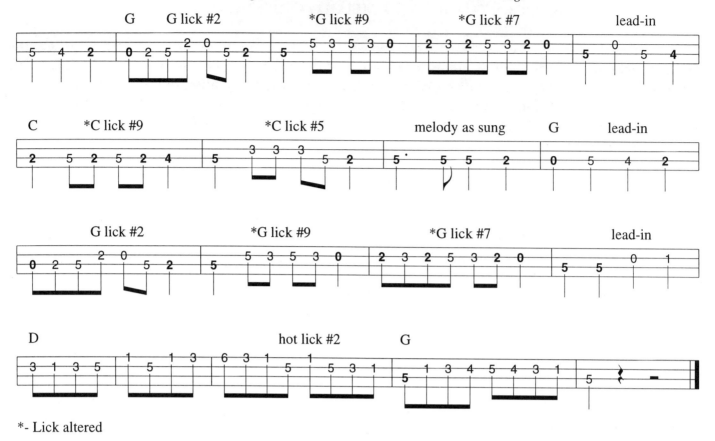

*- Lick altered

Exercise 21

INSERTING HOT LICKS

Return to your previous arrangements of Song Examples # 1, 2, 4, and 5. Insert hot licks in appropriate locations, particularly in the last line of song parts. *Because of the many choices and possibilities, there is no answer arrangement presented.*

Used sparingly, hot licks turn the heads of listeners and give you the reputation as a tasteful player whom other musicians enjoy playing with. Over-used, they can give you the reputation of a "hot-dog". Listen to the great players to get a sense of how to use hot licks. Also pay attention to the other musicians around you. What is an acceptable level of hot-lick playing in one jam session may be viewed as "hot dogging" in another.

Style

Some licks may not sound esthetically pleasing when combined. They may be totally different melodically, or too much the same. Certain licks may contain too much dissonance to be used adjacently, or a lick may not render a melody accurately enough to be acceptable to you. These are subjective decisions, and will take thoughtful experimentation to work out. This is part of the fun and the challenge in becoming an accomplished player. This is also how your personal style evolves. As you worked through the exercises in this book, you selected favorite licks and lick combinations. It is the things you incorporate, the things you leave out, and your level of execution that make your playing unique.

Musicians are like snowflakes - there are no two alike. Even two mandolinists who play the same arrangement at the same tempo on the same mandolin will sound different, because of subtle differences in timing, emphasis, and level of execution. These differences are what influences your style. The more you experiment and practice, the more your personal style will emerge. The diligent application of the concepts presented here will result in much more than the ability to play by ear - it will result in your developing a style that is unique.

Beyond Licks

In order to work out a solo like the one on the previous pages, you must do a great deal of experimenting. In time, you will learn your fingerboard and your ear will develop to the point that it will not be necessary to work out each measure one by one. It will no longer be necessary to write out your arrangements on paper. You will eventually be able to create arrangements "on the fly" simply by hearing or thinking of a melody or chord progression. The licks will become so internalized that for any given melody situation, an appropriate lick will simply "happen" as you play. You will then truly be playing by ear. Reaching this level is simply a result of working with these concepts so much that the whole process becomes subconscious. The only way to get there is through experience. This book can explain the process, but the progress in learning to teach yourself by ear takes place as a result of countless hours of experimentation and practice. So get busy!

Use the following blank staves to record revised arrangements from the exercises in this chapter or to experiment. Additional manuscript paper can be found at the end of other chapters or purchased at most music dealers.

Chapter 4

PLAYING IN DIFFERENT KEYS

In the previous exercises, we worked exclusively in the key of G major, a very popular key for music styles that include the mandolin. The key of G is also generally considered to be one of the easier keys to play in - there are many open string G scale notes, and the three basic chords can be formed as two-finger formations if the student is not ready for three or four-finger formations. We also limited the examples and exercises to one key because of the amount of conceptual information covered. Learning to identify chord relationships is especially difficult if each new example is in a different key. Working in one key allowed you to get a stronger sense of the "home base" quality of the 1 note and 1 chord so you would have a reference point from which to compare melody notes and chords you are trying to identify.

In this chapter, however, there will be no new information about chord progressions. You will simply be asked to put the previous information to work and gain experience learning songs by ear in some of the other popular keys. This will be much easier to do if you understand the number system, explained in Chapter 1. Studying the number system will lead to a real working understanding of chord progressions. It will show you that the concepts and relationships discussed earlier are true for all keys, and that you do not need to learn these concepts all over again every time you are faced with a new key. The number system is like a root language, and the various keys are like derivative languages. If you understand the number system, you can easily interpret the different keys in the letter system. If you are unsure about the number system, it may be a good idea to review Chapter 1 before learning songs in these unfamiliar keys.

The licks shown in Chapter 3 are moveable licks. That means they are mostly "closed position" licks - the only open strings used are ones that can be played by the index finger as a lick is moved up the fingerboard. The "shape" of the lick does not change as it is moved up or down the fingerboard, except when a note has to be altered to conform to the key at hand, or when you choose to play a fretted note on the adjacent open string, or an open string note on the adjacent fretted string. Though this makes moveable licks easily transposable to other keys, some of the transposed licks may actually be more difficult to play than first position licks you already know that contain more open string notes. This is especially true for the keys of B♭, B, and F. In these keys, using only the moveable licks from Chapter 3 may result in arrangements that contain virtually no open strings. In these keys, it will sometimes be easier to use licks you already know or create your own licks, guided by the melody of the song at hand. Another way to make these keys easier to navigate is to use a greater ratio of fill licks, altered to include the proper melody notes. You may choose to use only three or four moveable licks in a given song, mixed in with a generous portion of "generic" fill licks and phrasing licks. As with all "ear" playing, trial-and-error experimentation is necessary to create acceptable arrangements that are within your capabilities.

Vertical Transposing

In learning the preceding G, C and D licks, you have seen how one note sequence can be used in many different chord situations. The entire group of notes is simply shifted up or down in pitch until it fits the desired chord situation. We will call changing a phrase or entire song to another chord or key by moving it up or down the fingerboard *vertical transposing*.

We will use the 'G' tag lick to demonstrate. Suppose you want to use this lick in an 'A' situation. The A note, A scale, and **A** chord are one whole step, (two frets) higher in pitch than the G note, G scale, and **G** chord. To vertically transpose a 'G' lick to 'A', simply move all the notes up the fingerboard two frets. To use the lick in a 'B' situation, move it two more frets up the fingerboard. Because of the naturally-occurring half-step between the notes B and C, move it up only *one* fret to transpose to 'C'.

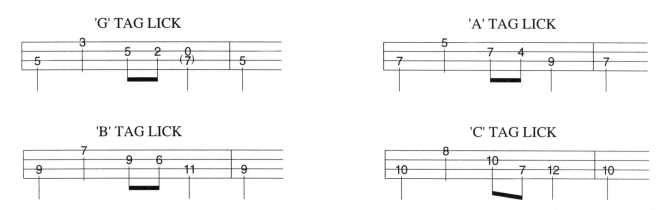

'G' TAG LICK   'A' TAG LICK

'B' TAG LICK   'C' TAG LICK

Of course you can also move licks down the fingerboard to transpose to a lower chord or key, as long as you have enough space on the fingerboard.

Fretted String Versus Open String

Sometimes after you transpose a lick, you will find it easier to locate certain fretted notes instead on an adjacent open string, or a note previously found on an open string must instead be played as a fretted note on the adjacent string. This will cause you to change the "shape" of the lick, and it will usually be necessary to change the fingering as well. Still, each note in the lick maintains the same relative pitch to the other notes. The lick has not changed musically, but the way you play it is different. This can be easily seen in the example below, because though the tablature looks different in the two examples, the 'A' tag lick sounds exactly like the closed position 'A' tag lick above. It is, however, much easier to perform.

'G' TAG LICK   'G' TAG, LICK TRANSPOSED TO 'A'
NOTES ALTERED

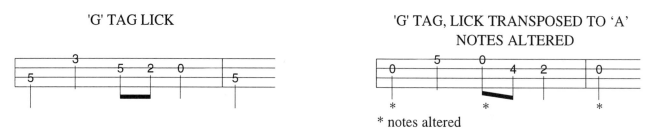

* notes altered

Running Out of Vertical Fingerboard Space

If you are transposing a lick down in pitch, you may occasionally run out of vertical fingerboard space - the transposed lick may contain notes that are below the low G note which is the lowest note on the mandolin. If only one or two notes are affected, you may be able to replace the affected notes without drastically changing the sound of the lick. If not, it will be necessary to choose another lick.

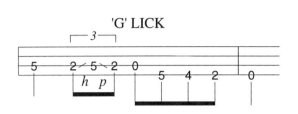

'G' LICK

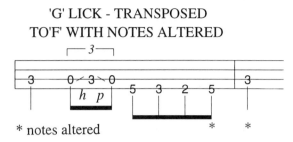

'G' LICK - TRANSPOSED
TO 'F' WITH NOTES ALTERED

* notes altered

You will rarely run out of fingerboard space when transposing a lick by moving it up the fingerboard, but because position changes may be too difficult to execute quickly or because of intonation problems, you may wish to choose another lick instead of the transposed lick.

Transposing Entire Arrangements Vertically

The same principles that apply to transposing licks apply to entire arrangements. To transpose a song up or down in pitch a short distance (one to five frets), move all chord positions and notes up or down the fingerboard. The following is an arrangement of the Sample Song *Worried Man Blues* from page 60 transposed vertically from the key of G to the key of A:

Worried Man Blues, Transposed Vertically From the Key of 'G' to the Key of 'A'

This arrangement can be heard on the demonstration recording.

65

Exercise 22

TRANSPOSING AN ARRANGEMENT VERTICALLY

Transpose your arrangement of Song Example #5 (page 49) from the key of G to the key of A. Use the blank staves below to record your arrangement. *Answer arrangement appears on page 94.*

Song Example #5 - Transposed Vertically From the Key of G to the Key of A
Note - The key of A is commonly considered the correct key for this song.

verse:

chorus:

Transposing to "Non-Natural" Chords and Keys

To transpose a lick or arrangement to a "sharp chord" or "sharp key", simply move it up the fingerboard one fret. For example, to play a 'G#' lick, move any 'G' lick up one fret:

To transpose a lick or arrangement to a "flat chord" or "flat key", move it down the fingerboard one fret. For example, to play a 'B♭' lick, move any 'B' lick down one fret:

Again, remember the naturally-occurring half-steps between B and C and between E and F. If you move a 'C' lick down a fret, you would call it a 'B' lick, not a 'C♭' lick. If you move an 'F' lick down a fret, you would call it an 'E' lick, not an 'F♭' lick. Conversely, If you move a 'B' lick up a fret, it becomes a 'C' lick, not a 'B#' lick. If you move an 'E' lick up a fret, it is called an 'F' lick, not an 'E#' lick.

Horizontal Transposing

Mandolin strings are tuned at equal intervals - the interval from any string to the adjacent lower string is a fourth; from any string to the adjacent higher string is a fifth. Therefore, in addition to transposing vertically, licks can be also be moved *horizontally*, or *across* the fingerboard. Any chord or lick can be transposed an interval of a fourth by moving it over one string towards the bass (see 'G' to 'C' below). Any chord or lick can be transposed an interval of a fifth by simply moving it over one string towards the treble ('C' to 'G' is a fifth - simply reverse the direction of the shift below).

To play a 'D' tag lick, you could either move the 'C' tag lick *up* two frets or move the 'A' tag lick *across* the fingerboard one string towards the bass. The results are the same. To play an 'E' tag lick, you could either move the 'D' tag lick up two frets or move the 'B' tag lick across the fingerboard one string towards the bass. Again, the results are the same.

To play an 'F' tag lick, either move the 'E' tag lick up one fret (a half-step), or move the higher octave 'C' tag lick over one string towards the bass (not shown).

Running Out of Horizontal Fingerboard Space

If a lick includes notes on the first string and you choose to transpose it by moving it across the fingerboard toward the treble strings, you will not have access to the notes that were previously found on the first string. To preserve the sound of the lick, it may be necessary to find some or all of the notes "up the neck":

Conversely, if a lick contains notes on the fourth string and you transpose it by moving it across the fingerboard towards the bass strings, you will run out of strings in the other direction. But you cannot add notes to the mandolin fingerboard below the low G (open fourth string). You must either alter the sound of the lick by substituting other notes, or choose another lick which does not include fourth string notes:

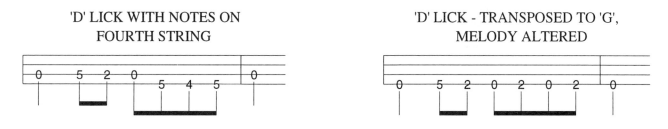

In these situations, you are altering the "shape" of the lick as played on the fingerboard. In some cases, the transposed lick will be more difficult to perform. It is up to you whether to learn the altered lick or to abandon it and use another lick which is easier to play.

Below is the previous arrangement of the sample song *Worried Man Blues* (page 65), transposed horizontally from the key of A to the key of D.

Worried Man Blues, Transposed Horizontally From the Key of 'A' to the Key of 'D'
This arrangement can be heard on the demonstration recording.

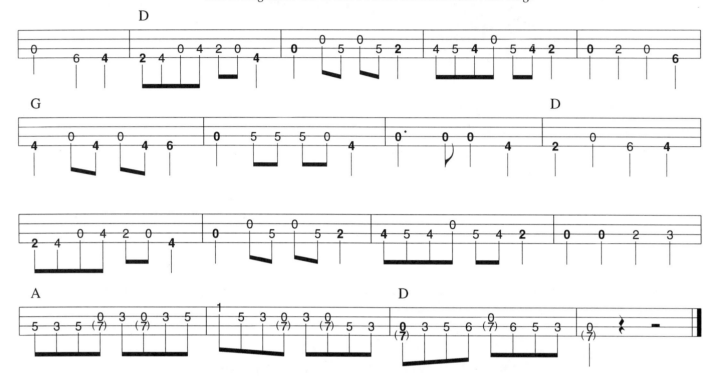

Exercise 23

TRANSPOSING AN ARRANGEMENT HORIZONTALLY

Transpose your arrangement of Song Example #5 (page 66) horizontally from the key of A to the key of D. Use the blank staves below to record your arrangement. *Answer arrangement appears on page 95.*

Song Example #5 - Transposed Horizontally From the Key of A to the Key of D

verse

chorus

Study the information in this section carefully. If you understand it, you can multiply your effective repertoire of licks many times over - many of the licks you know can be played in all twelve key or chord situations!

It is problem solving situations like these that help you become familiar with the fingerboard and facilitate quicker playing by ear. Another benefit is that many "happy mistakes" will occur, resulting in original licks that can become a part of your repertiore. This is part of the hands-on experience that no book or teacher can provide - you *must* experiment with your instrument.

Learning Songs in Different Keys

Now that you have a foundation in learning songs in the key of G and transposing licks and arrangements, you should be able to apply these principles to learning new songs in other keys. You learned Progressions #7 through #12 in the key of G major in Chapter 1. Keeping all examples in one key hopefully gave you a better sense of the different chord functions and chord relationships. But now we will learn these six songs in different keys in order to put to use the concepts discussed in this chapter.

The transposition chart on page 15 shows you the scales and basic chords in seven popular keys. If this information is clearly understood, you can transpose the licks in Chapter 3 to other keys. However, this may be too overwhelming for readers with limited experience. Therefore, the major scales and basic chords for other popular keys are presented in this chapter, making it easier to learn songs in these unfamiliar keys.

About the Arrangements

The twelve sample songs are performed with rhythm instruments and vocals. No introductory solos are used - all songs begin with the vocal melody so you will have an accurate melody source on which to base your solos. Due to space limitations, only a verse and a chorus and a mandolin solo will be presented. This is all you need to learn the melody by ear. In Song Examples #1 - #6, the mandolin solo is the final arrangement that appears in the *Answers to Exercises* section starting on page 91. In Song Examples #7 - #12, the author relies on the concepts explained in this book to create solos that you may compare to your solos or get ideas from.

These songs are recorded in split-channel format so you can eliminate the recorded mandolin part and join the band, playing your own arrangement. With the balance control of your stereo adjusted fully to the left, you can concentrate only on the rhythm instruments when identifying the chords. With the balance control adjusted fully to the right, you can focus only on the vocals when learning the melody. With the balance control in the middle position, you can listen for repetition in the melody to help you identify repeated chord sequences, or listen for repeated chord sequences to help you identify repetition in the melody. The split-channel format also makes it easier for you to study the sample arrangements and answers to exercises.

The Key of A Major

Below is the A major scale, the note palette for the key of A major. These are the A scale notes that are accessible in the first position, without having to move the left hand away from the nut. Familiarize yourself with these notes. The root notes (A notes) are circled. These are the notes that phrases and song parts will end on. Notice that the A major scale is simply the G major scale moved up in pitch a whole step, or two frets.

THE A MAJOR SCALE IN THE FIRST POSITION

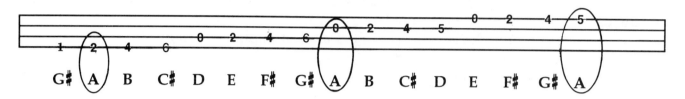

A MAJOR SCALE - FINGERBOARD CHART

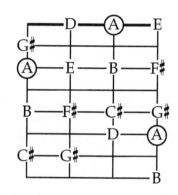

THE THREE BASIC CHORDS IN THE KEY OF A MAJOR

The 1 chord in the key of A major is the A chord.

The 4 chord in the key of A major is the D chord.

The 5 chord in the key of A major is the E (or E^7) chord.

THE SUPPORTING CHORDS IN THE KEY OF A MAJOR

The 2 chord in the key of A major is the B, Bm or B7 chord.

The 3 chord in the key of A major is the C♯, C♯m, or C♯7 chord.

The 6 chord in the key of A major is the F♯, F♯m, or F♯7 chord.

Exercise 24

CREATING A MELODY ARRANGEMENT BY EAR IN THE KEY OF A

Listen to Song Example #7 on the demonstration recording. (Not *Progression #7*, the instrumental example near the beginning of the recording, but the vocal arrangement which appears later in the recording). First identify the chords. Then use fill licks, phrasing licks, moveable licks, hot licks, original licks or licks you already know to create an arrangement by ear. It will often be necessary to transpose previously learned licks for use in unfamiliar chord situations. Use the blank staves below to write out your arrangement if you wish. Play the finished arrangement along with the demonstration recording to check your work. *Due to the many possibilities, there is no answer arrangement provided.*

Song Example #7

chorus:

verse:

The Key of B Major

Below is the B major scale, the note palette for the key of B major. These are the B scale notes that are accessible in the first position, without having to move the left hand away from the nut. Familiarize yourself with these notes. The root notes (B notes) are circled. These are the notes that phrases and song parts will end on. Notice that the B major scale is simply the A major scale moved up in pitch a whole step, or two frets.

THE B MAJOR SCALE IN THE FIRST POSITION

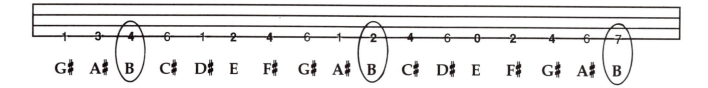

Bb MAJOR SCALE - FINGERBOARD CHART

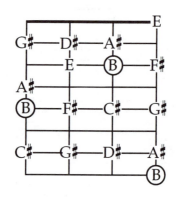

THE THREE BASIC CHORDS IN THE KEY OF B MAJOR

The 1 chord in the key of B major is the B chord.

The 4 chord in the key of B major is the E chord.

The 5 chord in the key of B major is the F♯ (or F♯7) chord.

THE SUPPORTING CHORDS IN THE KEY OF B MAJOR

The 2 chord in the key of B major is the C♯, C♯m or C♯7 chord.

The 3 chord in the key of B major is the D♯, D♯m, or D♯7 chord.

The 6 chord in the key of B major is the G♯, G♯m, or G♯7 chord.

Exercise 25

CREATING A MELODY ARRANGEMENT BY EAR IN THE KEY OF B

Listen to Song Example #8 on the demonstration recording. (Not *Progression #8*, the instrumental example near the beginning of the recording, but the vocal arrangement which appears later in the recording). First identify the chords. Then use fill licks, phrasing licks, moveable licks, hot licks, original licks or licks you already know to create an arrangement by ear. It will often be necessary to transpose previously learned licks for use in unfamiliar chord situations. Use the blank staves below to write out your arrangement if you wish. Play the finished arrangement along with the demonstration recording to check your work. *Due to the many possibilities, there is no answer arrangement provided.*

Song Example #8

chorus:

verse:

The Key of C Major

Below is the C major scale, the note palette for the key of C major. These are the C scale notes that are accessible in the first position, without having to move the left hand away from the nut. Familiarize yourself with these notes. The root notes (C notes) are circled. These are the notes that phrases and song parts will end on. Notice that the C major scale is simply the B major scale moved up in pitch a half step, or one fret.

THE C MAJOR SCALE IN THE FIRST POSITION

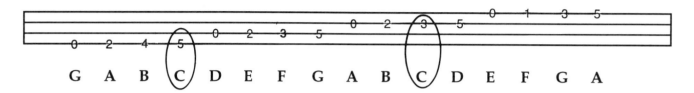

G   A   B   C   D   E   F   G   A   B   C   D   E   F   G   A

C MAJOR SCALE - FINGERBOARD CHART

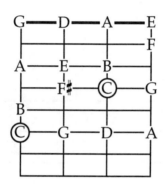

THE THREE BASIC CHORDS IN THE KEY OF C MAJOR

The 1 chord in the key of C major is the C chord.

The 4 chord in the key of C major is the F chord.

The 5 chord in the key of C major is the G (or G⁷) chord.

THE SUPPORTING CHORDS IN THE KEY OF B♭ MAJOR

The 2 chord in the key of C major is the D, Dm or D⁷ chord.

The 3 chord in the key of C major is the E, Em, or E⁷ chord.

The 6 chord in the key of C major is the A, Am, or A⁷ chord.

Exercise 26

CREATING A MELODY ARRANGEMENT BY EAR IN THE KEY OF C

Listen to Song Example #9 on the demonstration recording. (Not *Progression #9*, the instrumental example near the beginning of the recording, but the vocal arrangement which appears later in the recording). First identify the chords. Then use fill licks, phrasing licks, moveable licks, hot licks, original licks or licks you already know to create an arrangement by ear. It will often be necessary to transpose previously learned licks for use in unfamiliar chord situations. Use the blank staves below to write out your arrangement if you wish. Play the finished arrangement along with the demonstration recording to check your work. *Due to the many possibilities, there is no answer arrangement provided.*

Song Example #9

verse:

chorus:

The Key of D Major

Below is the D major scale, the note palette for the key of D major. These are the D scale notes that are accessible in the first position, without having to move the left hand away from the nut. Familiarize yourself with these notes. The root notes (D notes) are circled. These are the notes that phrases and song parts will end on. Notice that the D major scale is simply the C major scale moved up in pitch a whole step, or two frets.

THE D MAJOR SCALE IN THE FIRST POSITION

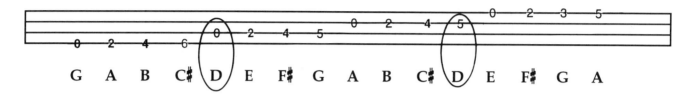

G A B C# D E F# G A B C# D E F# G A

D MAJOR SCALE - FINGERBOARD CHART

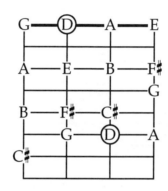

THE THREE BASIC CHORDS IN THE KEY OF D MAJOR

The 1 chord in the key of D major is the D chord.

The 4 chord in the key of D major is the G chord.

The 5 chord in the key of D major is the A (or A⁷) chord.

THE SUPPORTING CHORDS IN THE KEY OF D MAJOR

The 2 chord in the key of D major is the E, Em or E⁷ chord.

The 3 chord in the key of D major is the F#, F#m, or F#⁷ chord.

The 6 chord in the key of D major is the B, Bm, or B⁷ chord.

Exercise 27

CREATING A MELODY ARRANGEMENT BY EAR IN THE KEY OF D

Listen to Song Example #10 on the demonstration recording. (Not *Progression #10*, the instrumental example near the beginning of the recording, but the vocal arrangement which appears later in the recording). First identify the chords. Then use fill licks, phrasing licks, moveable licks, hot licks, original licks or licks you already know to create an arrangement by ear. It will often be necessary to transpose previously learned licks for use in unfamiliar chord situations. Use the blank staves below to write out your arrangement if you wish. Play the finished arrangement along with the demonstration recording to check your work. *Due to the many possibilities, there is no answer arrangement provided.*

Song Example #10

chorus:

verse:

The Key of E Major

Below is the E major scale, the note palette for the key of E major. These are the E scale notes that are accessible in the first position, without having to move the left hand away from the nut. Familiarize yourself with these notes. The root notes (E notes) are circled. These are the notes that phrases and song parts will end on. Notice that the E major scale is simply the F major scale moved up in pitch a half step, or one fret.

THE E MAJOR SCALE IN THE FIRST POSITION

G#   A   B   C#   D#   E   F#   G#   A   B   C#   D#   E   F#   G#   A

E MAJOR SCALE - FINGERBOARD CHART

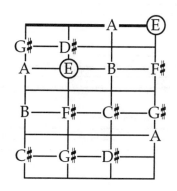

THE THREE BASIC CHORDS IN THE KEY OF E MAJOR

The 1 chord in the key of E major is the E chord.

The 4 chord in the key of E major is the A chord.

The 5 chord in the key of E major is the B (or B⁷) chord.

THE SUPPORTING CHORDS IN THE KEY OF E MAJOR

The 2 chord in the key of E major is the F#, F#m, or F#⁷ chord.

The 3 chord in the key of E major is the G#, G#m, or G#⁷ chord.

The 6 chord in the key of E major is the C#, C#m, or C#⁷ chord.

Exercise 28

CREATING A MELODY ARRANGEMENT BY EAR IN THE KEY OF E

Listen to Song Example #11 on the demonstration recording. (Not *Progression #11*, the instrumental example near the beginning of the recording, but the vocal arrangement which appears later in the recording). First identify the chords. Then use fill licks, phrasing licks, moveable licks, hot licks, original licks or licks you already know to create an arrangement by ear. It will often be necessary to transpose previously learned licks for use in unfamiliar chord situations. Use the blank staves below to write out your arrangement if you wish. Play the finished arrangement along with the demonstration recording to check your work. *Due to the many possibilities, there is no answer arrangement provided.*

Song Example #11

chorus/verse:

The Key of F Major

Below is the F major scale, the note palette for the key of F major. These are the F scale notes that are accessible in the first position, without having to move the left hand away from the nut. Familiarize yourself with these notes. The root notes (F notes) are circled. These are the notes that phrases and song parts will end on. Notice that the F major scale is simply the D major scale moved up in pitch a whole step, or two frets.

THE F MAJOR SCALE IN THE FIRST POSITION

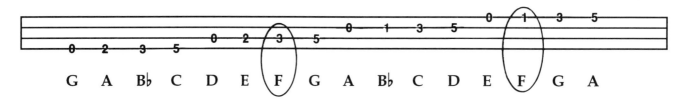

F MAJOR SCALE - FINGERBOARD CHART

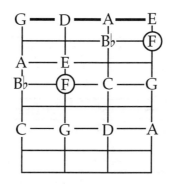

THE THREE BASIC CHORDS IN THE KEY OF F MAJOR

The 1 chord in the key of F major is the F chord.

The 4 chord in the key of F major is the Bb chord.

The 5 chord in the key of F major is the C (or C⁷) chord.

THE SUPPORTING CHORDS IN THE KEY OF F MAJOR

The 2 chord in the key of F major is the G, Gm or G⁷ chord.

The 3 chord in the key of F major is the A, Am, or A⁷ chord.

The 6 chord in the key of F major is the D, Dm, or D⁷ chord.

Exercise 29

CREATING A MELODY ARRANGEMENT BY EAR IN THE KEY OF F

Listen to Song Example #12 on the demonstration recording. (Not *Progression #12*, the instrumental example near the beginning of the recording, but the vocal arrangement which appears later in the recording). First identify the chords. Then use fill licks, phrasing licks, moveable licks, hot licks, original licks or ones you already know to create an arrangement by ear. It will often be necessary to transpose previously learned licks for use in unfamiliar chord situations. Use the blank staves below to write out your arrangement if you wish. Play the finished arrangement along with the demonstration recording to check your work. *Due to the many possibilities, there is no answer arrangement provided.*

Song Example #12

verse:

chorus:

Use the following blank staves to record arrangements or experiment. Additional manuscript paper can be purchased at most music dealers.

Page 9, Exercise 1

DETERMINING METER

1 4/4	4 4/4	7 4/4	10 4/4
2 4/4	5 4/4	8 4/4	11 4/4
3 3/4	6 3/4	9 4/4	12 4/4

Page 10, Exercise 2

LOCATING SIMPLE CHORD CHANGES

Progression #1:
Meter:____4/4____

Verse/Chorus:

x   x

x   x   x   x

Progression #2:
Meter:____4/4____

Verse:

x   x   x

x   x

Chorus:

x   x   x   x   x

x   x   x

Progression #3:
Meter:____3/4____

Verse/Chorus:

x   x   x   x

x   x   x   x   x

LOCATING SPLIT-BAR CHORD CHANGES

Progression #4:
Meter:_____4/4_____

Verse:

| x | | | | | | | | x | x | | | | | | x | x |

Chorus:

| | | | | | | | | x | x | | | | | | x | x |

Progression #5:
Meter:_____4/4_____

Verse:

| x | | | x | x | | | x | x | | | x | x | | x | x |

Chorus:

| | | | | | | x | x | | | | | | | x | x |

Progression #6:
Meter:_____3/4_____

Verse/Chorus:

| x | x | x | | | x | x | | x | | x | |

| x | | x | | | x | x | | | x | x | |

LEARNING "BASIC THREE" PROGRESSIONS BY EAR

Progression #1:
Meter:_____4/4_____

Verse/Chorus:

| G | | | | | | D | |

| G | | C | | D | | G | |

Progression #2:
Meter:_____

Verse/Chorus:

G				D		G	

			D		G	

Chorus:

C		G		C		G	D

G				D		G	

Progression #3:
Meter:_____

Verse/Chorus:

G		C	G			D	

G		C	G		D	G	

Progression #4:
Meter:____4/4____

Verse:

G			D	G			D G

Chorus:

			D G				D G

Progression #5:
Meter:____4/4____

Verse:

G	C	G		D	G	C	G	D G

Chorus:

			D G				D G

Progression #6:
Meter:____3/4____

Verse/Chorus:

G C	G		D G	D	G

D	G		C G		D G

Page 21, Exercise 5

IDENTIFYING MAJOR, MINOR AND SEVENTH CHORD TYPES

1	C	11	C	21	B	31	C
2	A	12	A	22	A	32	B
3	B	13	B	23	C	33	A
4	A	14	C	24	B	34	B
5	C	15	A	25	A	35	C
6	C	16	B	26	A	36	A
7	A	17	A	27	C	37	B
8	B	18	C	28	B	38	B
9	A	19	C	29	B	39	C
10	A	20	B	30	A	40	A

Page 28, Exercise 6

LEARNING PROGRESSIONS CONTAINING ONE SUPPORTING CHORD

Progression #7:
Meter: 4/4
Key: G

Verse/Chorus:

G		F		G	D	G	

G		F		G	D	G	

Progression #8:
Meter: 4/4
Key: G

Verse/Chorus:

G				C		G	

C		G	Em	G	D	G	

Progression #9:
Meter: 4/4
Key: G

Verse:

G		C	G	C	G	A	D

G		C	G	C	G	D	G

Chorus:

C		G		D		G	

C		G		D		G	

LEARNING PROGRESSIONS CONTAINING TWO SUPPORTING CHORDS

Progression #10:
Meter: 4/4
Key: G

Verse/Chorus:

C		G		C		G	

	B7	C		G	D	G	

Progression #11:
Meter: 4/4
Key: G

Verse/Chorus:

G						D	

					D7	G	

						C	

		G	E7	A7	D7	G	

Progression #12:
Meter: 4/4
Key: G

Verse/Chorus:

G	E	A		D		G	

G	E	A		D		G	

Page 34. Exercise 8

IDENTIFYING SIMPLE MELODIES FROM MEMORY

Mary Had a Little Lamb

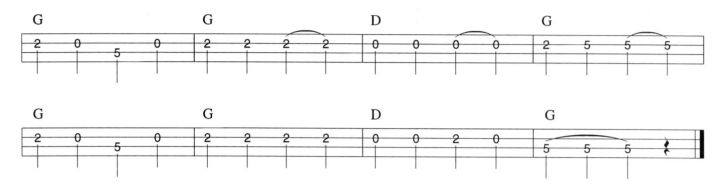

Skip to My Lou

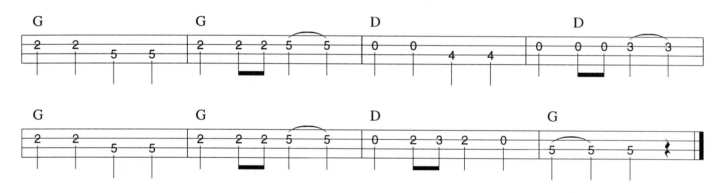

This Old Man (Knick-Knack, Paddy-Whack)

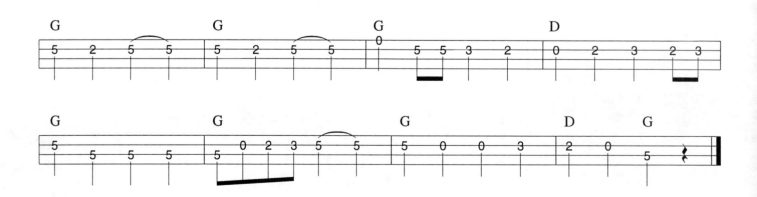

Page 37, Exercise 9

LOCATING FIRST-BEAT MELODY NOTES

Song Example # 1 - First-beat Melody Notes

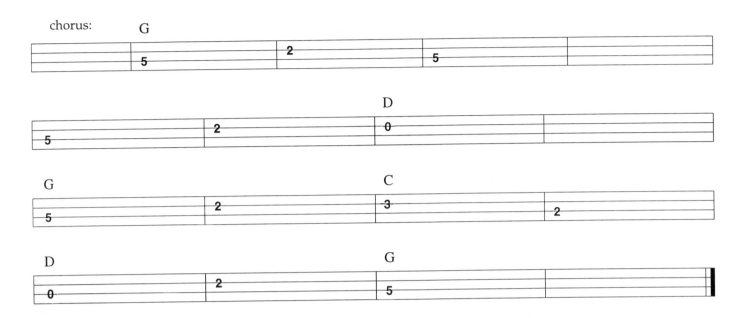

Page 38, Exercise 10

USING FILL LICKS

Song Example # 1 - First-beat Melody Notes with Fill Licks

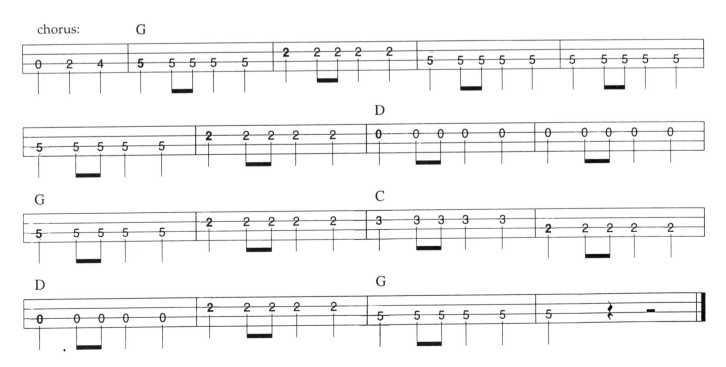

Page 41, Exercise 11

USING PHRASING LICKS

Song Example # 1 - First-beat Melody Notes with Phrasing Licks

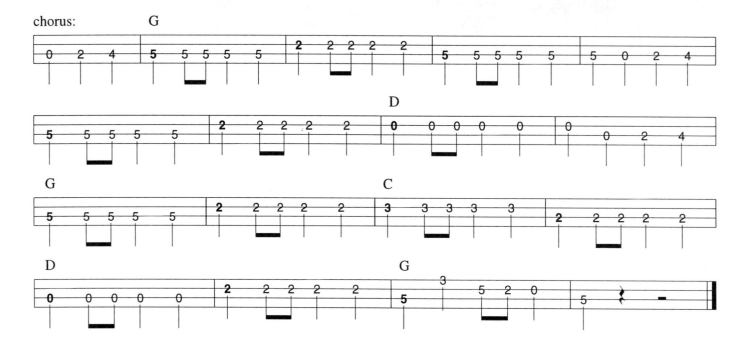

Page 43, Exercise 12

CREATING A FIRST-BEAT AND LAST-BEAT MELODY ORIENTED ARRANGEMENT

Song Example # 1 - First-beat and Last-beat Melody Notes with Phrasing Licks

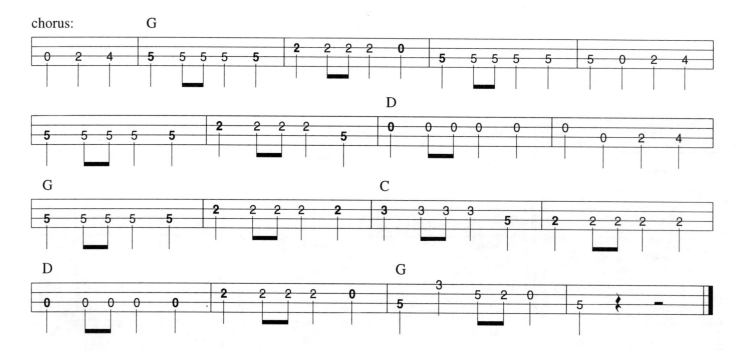

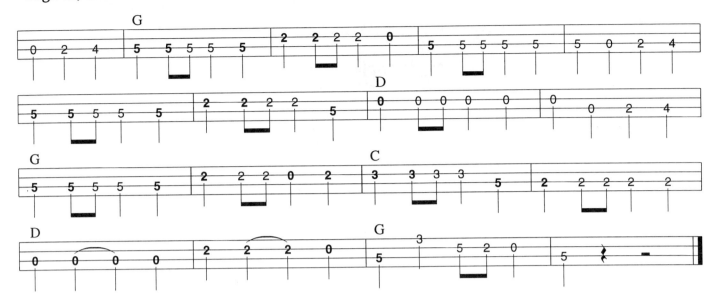

Page 44, Ex. 14 - CREATING A MELODY ARRANGEMENT BY EAR "FROM SCRATCH" S. E. #2

CREATING A MELODY ORIENTED SOLO IN 3/4 TIME

Song Example # 3 - Melody

Song Example # 3 - Melody Oriented Solo with Phrasing Licks

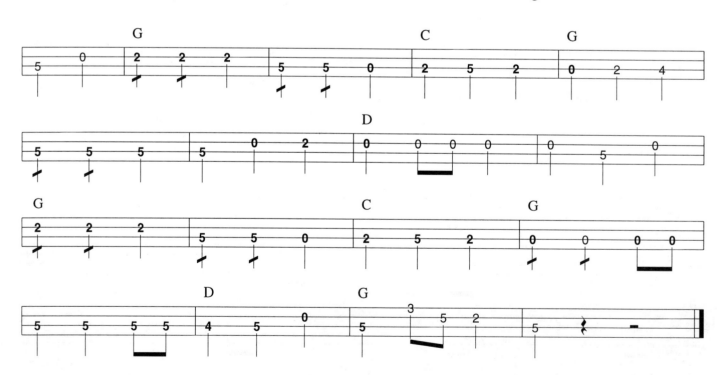

LEARNING QUICKLY-CHANGING MELODIES BY EAR

Song Example # 4 - Melody-Oriented Solo

Song Example #5 - Melody-Oriented Solo

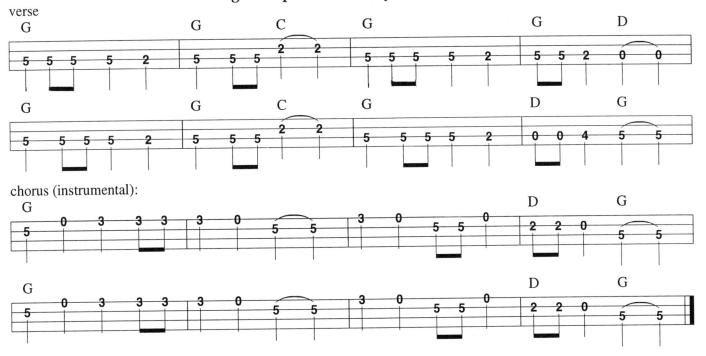

Page 50, Exercise 16c

Song Example # 6

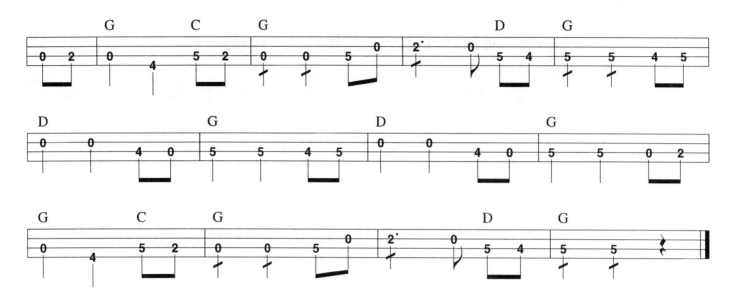

Exercises 17 - 21

Due to the many choices and possibilities, there are no definitive answers to exercises #17 - #21. You may check your arrangements by playing along with the recording, the balance control of your stereo adjusted fully to the left so you can hear the chord accompaniment.

Page 66, Exercise 22

TRANSPOSING AN ARRANGEMENT VERTICALLY

Song Example #5 - Transposed Vertically From the Key of G to the Key of A

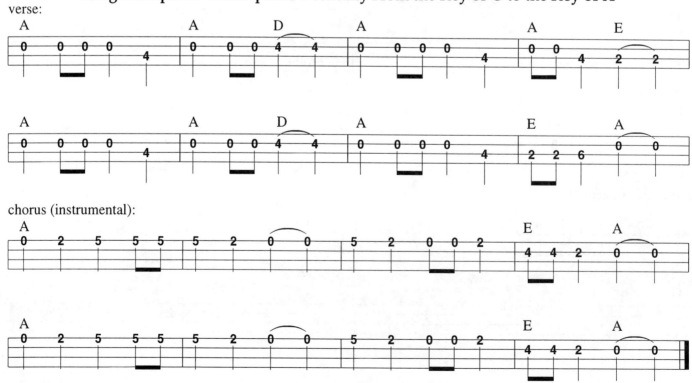

TRANSPOSING AN ARRANGEMENT HORIZONTALLY

Song Example #5 - Transposed Horizontally From the Key of A to the Key of D

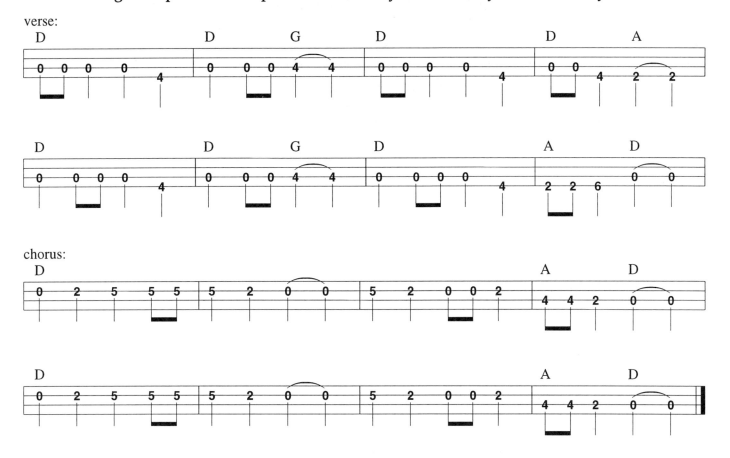

Exercises #24 - #29

Due to the many choices and possibilities, there are no specific answers to exercises 24 - 29. You may check your arrangements by playing along with the demonstration recording with the balance control of your stereo adjusted fully to the left so you can hear the chord accompaniment.

Titles of Song Examples

The titles of the song examples were intentionally withheld so an arrangement you may already know would not influence your learning the Song Example entirely by ear. The titles appear below.

Song Ex.#1 - *Roll in My Sweet Baby's Arms*
Song Ex. #2 - *Columbus Stockade Blues*
Song Ex.#3- *All The Good Times are Past and Gone*
Song Ex. #4 - *Sourwood Mountain*
Song Ex. #5- *Cotton - Eyed Joe*
Song Ex. #6 - *Rock of Ages*

Song Ex. #7 - *Yonder Stands Little Maggie*
Song Ex. #8 - *Roll On, Buddy, Roll On*
Song Ex. #9 - *Redwing*
Song Ex. #10- *Make Me A Pallet on Your Floor*
Song Ex. #11 - *Bill Bailey, Please Come Home*
Song Ex. #12 - *Salty Dog Blues*

Other Publications by Jack Hatfield

BLUEGRASS BANJO METHOD

A four-volume series that takes the student from ground zero to advanced level. "...Still the best book on the market for beginners."-*Banjo Newsletter*, Feb 1994. "...It's more capable of {teaching the beginner} the basics of Scruggs style banjo than any other manual..."*Bluegrass Unlimited*, Jan. 1985. BOOK 1- *Basic Rolls and Left Hand Techniques*. BOOK 2-*Playing in 3/4 time, Playing Up the Neck, Playing in Different Keys, Learning the Fingerboard*. BOOK 3-*Backup Techniques*. BOOK-4 *Advanced Soloing Techniques*. Each book includes slow-fast cassette tape with banjo on one channel and rhythm on the other.

RHYTHM TRAX™ Practice Tapes

Guitar, mandolin and bass play rhythm to the most popular bluegrass instrumentals while you play lead. Slow/fast. Ten tunes on each tape. Companion books available with musical notation and/or tablature for banjo, guitar, fiddle and mandolin (See **TUNES**™ books ad below). Four tapes available:

BANJO TUNES - VOLUME 1
BANJO TUNES - VOLUME 2
FIDDLE TUNES - VOLUME 1
FIDDLE TUNES - VOLUME 2

TUNES™ Books

Each book contains tablature and/or musical notation for ten popular bluegrass instrumentals. Coincides with the **RHYTHM TRAX**™ tapes listed above.

BANJO TUNES - VOLUME 1
BANJO TUNES - VOLUME 2
FIDDLE TUNES - VOLUME 1
FIDDLE TUNES - VOLUME 2
FIDDLE TUNES FOR BANJO - VOLUME 1
FIDDLE TUNES FOR BANJO - VOLUME 2

FIDDLE TUNES FOR MANDOLIN - VOLUME 1
FIDDLE TUNES FOR MANDOLIN - VOLUME 2
FIDDLE TUNES FOR GUITAR - VOLUME 1
FIDDLE TUNES FOR GUITAR - VOLUME 2

HOW TO PLAY BY EAR

An in-depth look at chords and chord progressions: Scales, chord construction, chord progression logic, chord functions, identifying chord types, using process of elimination and the laws of probability, the number system, a step-by-step procedure to learn chord progressions by ear. For all musicians, songwriters, and composers, any level, any instrument. Includes demo cassette with ear training exercises, split-channel recording. 175 pages.

YOU CAN TEACH YOURSELF® BANJO BY EAR

Unique book by Jack Hatfield that shows how to learn both progressions and melodies by ear using a step-by-step procedure. Book (MB95424), Cassette (MB95424C), and CD (95424CD) available from Mel Bay Publications, Inc.

ROUNDER OLD-TIME MUSIC FOR BANJO

Transcriptions and arrangements from the CD *Rounder Old-Time Music*. Book (MB95730) and CD (95774CD) available from Mel Bay Publications, Inc.

HATFIELD MUSIC CATALOG

Full descriptions & photos of Hatfield Music publications and products. Send long S.A.S.E.:
HATFIELD MUSIC P.O. BOX 6263 KNOXVILLE, TN 37914 Phone/Fax 1-800-426-8744
email: hatfield@tdsnet.com • **Website:** http://hmi.homewood.net/hatmusic